Towards Innovation in Legal Educati

Towards Innovation in Legal Education

Pasquale Policastro (Ed.)

eleven international publishing

Published, sold and distributed by Eleven International Publishing
P.O. Box 85576
2508 CG The Hague
The Netherlands
Tel.: +31 70 33 070 33
Fax: +31 70 33 070 30
e-mail: sales@budh.nl
www.elevenpub.com

Sold and distributed in USA and Canada
International Specialized Book Services
920 NE 58th Avenue, Suite 300
Portland, OR 97213-3786, USA
Tel: 1-800-944-6190 (toll-free)
Fax: +1-503-280-8832
orders@isbs.com
www.isbs.com

Eleven International Publishing is an imprint of Boom uitgevers Den Haag.

Printed with the Support of the European Commission, Education and Culture DG, Lifelong Learning Program, MENU FOR JUSTICE – TOWARDS AN EUROPEAN CURRICULUM STUDIORUM ON JUDICIAL STUDIES. Contract number – 2009 – 3675 / 001- 001, Project number – 156171-LLP-1-2009-1- IT-ERASMUS ENWA

Cover image: Luca Giordano, Fresco in the Palazzo Medici Ricardi in Florence, Justice, 1684–1686

ISBN 978-94-6236-057-0
ISBN 978-94-6094-757-5 (E-book)

Printed in The Netherlands

Table of Contents

Introduction by the Editor

Some years ago, in the spring of 2002, I had the occasion to write on a study about fundamental rights in the Polish democratic transition[1] that European constitutionalism developed through a continuous mediation between 'what is old' and 'what is new'. This mediation led, in the course of history, to the establishment of all the institutions and the legal remedies addressed to make sure an indispensable standard of freedom and equality for each individual at the same conditions as others. The role of the lawyer – to mediate between potentially contrasting situations – however, maintains its fundamental core, but evolved over time. As the constitutional institutions developed and the terms of the interaction between different legal orders manifested a growing complexity, the mediation of the lawyer required a more active search and equilibrium between the different individual and collective positions in all the situations in which law had to be produced and applied. The importance of such a search was especially noteworthy in all situations where law was challenged by political, social and economic difficulties. However, the achievement of the demanded mediation required that the lawyer could have a direct representation of the state of the art of constitutionalism, which is by itself funded on a plurality of categories of equilibrium,[2] and when the lawyer could be in the position to adequately purport such an understanding. Our explanation of the democratic transition in Poland was then related to the result of our enquiry that in Poland lawyers had the possibility, even during the period when political pluralism was not guaranteed and freedoms were tamed, to develop a representation of law on the basis of the foundations of constitutionalism. Furthermore, lawyers had, in some of the key moments of Polish constitutional history, and especially in the period which led to the transition of the

1 'Prawa podstawowe w demokratycznych transformacjach ustrojowych', *Polski przykład*, Lublin 2002, p. 471 *et seq*.

2 For what concerns our approach to constitutionalism, we consider it is related to some classes of questions concerning: (1) the constitutionalism as a rule of the political power, (2) how the development of a substantive constitutional framework takes place as a rule of law, and (3) the levels of interdependence between legal subjects and legal orders representing them. These questions relate, in our conception, to the orders of complexity of the idea of constitutionalism. The said questions may be approached by means of the 'paradigms of constitutionalism'. In one of the last versions to our approach we have been considering them as (1) the relation between the description of the existential manifestation of the person and of the modalities of their protection, (2) the relation between representation and participation; (3) the relation between norms and the sense they acquire through the interaction, in time and space, between legal subjects, between communities and between legal orders. *See* P. Policastro, 'Constitutionalism, Comparison, Complexity: Prolegomena on Liberty and the Use of Language for a Predictive Theory of Law', *in* P. Policastro & E. Castorina (Eds.), *Liberty and Language. The Global Dimension of European Constitutional Integration*, Torino, 2011, p. 21. For a first conception of such a problem, you can see P. Policastro, 'Political Parties, Participation and Representation Face to Globalisation, European Integration and Democratic Transition', *in* M. Granat, P. Policastro & J. Sobczak (Eds.), *Partie polityczne we współczesnym konstytucjonalizmie*, Lublin 2001; the first accomplished use of our approach to the paradigms of constitutionalism has taken place in 'Prawa podstawowe [. . .]', note 1.

end of the 1980s, and followed it, the authority to purport the constitutional transformation. Ten years after writing the pages just summarized, I had the opportunity to present the concluding speech in a conference on 'The constitutional process in the Mediterranean basin',[3] which took place in Istanbul. Again, I stressed that the lawyers, in the different countries of the region, had the knowledge and the ability to have a clear representation of constitutionalism. The problematic question was whether the lawyers had the authority to purport their opinions in a way that they could be accepted. My conclusion was that the development of the transnational contacts between the societies may have had an important role in a new understanding of constitution joining peace with the protection of the existential manifestation of the person in a context where legal orders are interdependent.

The motor of such transformation should be, as usual, cultural. The period between the above-mentioned transition in Central and Eastern Europe opened a number of waves of transformation, the first of which has been a transformation of the process of European integration, and the last one we know is the one in the Mediterranean. All these processes require a lawyer who is in a position to preserve the equilibrium between the protection of the person and the development of public duties, having simultaneously both sufficient knowledge and authority. If we look at these considerations in the perspective of history, we see that, independently from the geopolitical perspective in which it is presented, the transition from the antiquities to the modern construction of law and politics has started to a significant extent from the diffusion of a specific form of reasoning, the recursive reasoning, from Indian and Arab higher education institutes, to Europe.[4] This process led to the approach to reasoning, which created an identity of the European university: A reasoning able to guard an equilibrium between moral understanding and understanding by means of reason, and which permitted the development of the modern understanding of law in close relation with constitutionalism.
These reflections permit to acknowledge the central role of what is taught at university, in a way that is consistent with, but that at the same time goes beyond, the reflections presented by the authors of this volume. At the same time, we can see that, similarly as in the long transition from antiquity and Hellenism to modernity, the truly meaningful aspect was how ideas could circulate and be implemented. This aspect, the circulation of ideas, became the deciding factor whenever law and the founding principles of the civilization were challenged. Innovation in legal education appears therefore strongly related to the adequate circulation of thoughts and methods, permitting the lawyer to understand the

3 P. Policastro, 'L'Espace constitutionnel Pan-Européen et Mediterrenéen et nouvelle supra-nationalité', *Anayasa Hukuku Dergisi/Journal of Constitutional Law/Revue de droit constitutionnel* 2/2012, forthcoming.
4 C.I. Beckwith, *Warriors of the Cloisters. The Central Asian Origins of Science in the Medieval World*, Princeton and Oxford, 2012.

values beneath each problem of mediation and to propose an answer with sufficient authority and intensity.

The project 'Menu for Justice – Toward a European Curriculum Studiorum on Judicial Studies' created the opportunity to confront and to debate on how and in which way legal education could meet the new challenges of mediation. The results it produced ranged beyond the partner universities and became, also by means of formal and informal dissemination activities, a part of the life of the partner universities and the different academic agendas, in and outside of European Union, which are keeping close contacts with the different participants of the project.
The aim of the book is to present proposals and suggestions related to how legal training may support the development of adequate knowledge, professional skills and competence of the lawyer to deal with the present transformation and challenges. Its structure, articulated in four chapters, reflects a part of the dissemination process of the project 'Menu for Justice' oriented to develop guidelines for a European curriculum of studies. Therefore it tries to show why innovation in legal education is needed, what the current trends and difficulties are, what are the opportunities offered by innovation and in what way higher education institutions may generate and implement innovation. It attempts to do so through a number of short articles, presenting the perspective of scholars who either have been participating in its activities or who have been involved in the debate by means of the dissemination activities of 'Menu for Justice'. The chapters do not intend to present by any means a comprehensive analysis of the presented issues, but intend to offer a reflection on the importance of innovation to achieve a growing development of a European space of higher education, especially concerning legal education. Each of the chapters considers a different set of questions that address the new demands for legal training. The dynamic character of the demand for legal training is considered in Part I 'Legal Transformations and Innovation'. A first consideration is that the sources of the demand of innovation are manifold. They can be the activities of the jurisdiction considered in its systemic dimension (see Chapter 1 by Banaszak), as well as the need to think of the reconstruction of the legal order by legal scholars and judges of the supreme jurisdictions (see Chapter 2 by Arnold). There can also be the enterprises, in their endeavour to adapt themselves to the new legal and societal demands, in a situation characterized by a very significant transnational transformation of the economic sphere (see Chapter 3 by Makowicz). The case of Turkey has also been presented in Chapter 4, where, following the interaction of the national order with the judicature of the European Convention of Human Rights, scholars and civil society came to demand a higher consideration and a better training of lawyers, especially of judges and prosecutors, however within a significant structural resistance. The complexity in the demand of innovation relates to a complexity of the sources of innovation. Innovation clearly reflects the open characteristics of the interacting systems

within which societal transformations take place. This poses the problem of language, which may overshadow the different national experiences. To this extent, programmatic documents, such as the ones relating to the development of the European space of higher education, as well as other institutional initiatives, when they are put into practice, shall be integrated by activities of the national authorities and by the universities. Therefore, the networking and the communication between scholars joining research and higher education are important reference systems of evaluation. A very important outcome of the project 'Menu For Justice' has been the possibility of a frank and personal dialogue, together with an explanation of the reasons justifying different solutions and different approaches to innovation.

The importance of the dialogue between universities, institutions, scholars and teachers, students and civil society at large can generate a strong potential for innovation, as we can see in Part II. The core issue of this part is the development of legal studies permitting to the future lawyers to achieve high standards of knowledge, skills and competences.[5] The symbiosis between the first and the second level of studies, the integration between purely legal disciplines, interdisciplinary and complementary disciplines, as well as joining the different methodologies, permit to consider the importance of the context of the learning process. These questions may be approached in different ways. However, the need for a constant enrichment of the curricula of higher legal education to meet the growing interaction between the different fields of knowledge has also continuously been enriched by a clearly comparative dimension. Students should be taught to use information and synthesize it, in a way crossing different cultural and disciplinary contexts (see Chapter 5 by Berkmanas). Furthermore, the societal transformation of the community where higher studies are provided also needs to involve, to a greater extent, all the participants in the learning process. In particular, a more active involvement of the students appears suitable and gives good results. The Danish experience described by Ole Hammerslev in Chapter 6 shows an interesting convergence between the general trends in the evolution of the learning process, aiming to join knowledge, skill and competence with the needs related to the enlargement and the transformation of the social base acceding to higher education. The other chapters presented highlight, however, that the search for a good model of legal studies, conforming to the European trends, and answering at best the needs for well-trained lawyers, requires also good and loyal cooperation between the universities and

5 Recommendation of the European Parliament and of the Council of 23 April 2008 on the establishment of the European Qualifications Framework for lifelong learning, Official Journal C 111, 06/05/2008, p. 000-0007. See especially Annex I containing the 'definitions', according to which 'For the purposes of the Recommendation, the definitions which apply are the following: [. . .] (f) "learning outcomes" means statements of what a learner knows, understands and is able to do on completion of a learning process, which are defined in terms of knowledge, skills and competence'.

the ministries. For example, the Polish authors express worries about the development of unexpected and simplified legal studies, where the temporary interests of the university to increase their turnover appear to prevail over other considerations on the quality of the legal studies (Chapters 8 and 9 by Bałaban and Andrzejewski). Furthermore, they also manifest fears for the uncertain legislative frame of transformation within which legal education evolves, for the insufficient role granted to the public debate, as well as for the process of deregulation of the legal profession together with the illusion that lowering the condition for the access to the legal profession may create new jobs (Bałaban). The answer to the problem is surely connected with the importance of a wider and clearer debate, which takes into account from one side the importance of European integration, but furthermore permits to find the different paths of adaptation involving universities, government and the other social forces – a debate, we would add, which gives the right importance to the development of a European space of higher education. Here the consideration that a growing networking between the universities may be the prelude for a growing acknowledgement of the need to guarantee a good quality of the studies, in accordance with similar and clear principles, is of fundamental importance for the whole process of European integration. This dialogue, nevertheless, shall always take into account the specific needs of legal education, which is the development of an adequate ground for debating (Andrzejewski).

Innovation shall also take into account that, within the social and technological changes that take place, we have some basic characteristics of the legal profession which remain unchanged; such changes also create, nevertheless, the need for new legal professions. A very important case is that, to permit the safe and efficient functioning of justice, it is of key importance today the development of a new figure of lawyer, who shall take care of court administration. Part III is indeed dedicated to the development of such a new profession of lawyer. Indeed, the correct functioning of all the activities provided by a court and related to a trial, including also the relation of the courts with the mass media and the public, requires specific skills and knowledge, and a related research activity, which is not covered by the knowledge needed to perform the traditional professions of judge and prosecutor (see Chapter 9 by Langbroek). A very important corollary of these statements is that innovation in legal education is also related to the search of emerging professional figures in the field of law. The case of the court administration is especially important, and for this reason, it is worth taking into account the innovation in the curricula to adapt to such needs (see Chapter 10 by Lepore). However, the enlargement of the needs in legal education requires the development of a space of experimentation and adaptation to the changing reality. These aspects are treated in Part IV. Indeed the manifold aspects of European integration require a European lawyer who shall be aware both of the specific character of the process of European Integration and of the different national perspectives which merge into it. For this reason innovation may mean also the transformation of the university into a network, providing multilingual legal education based upon a full mobility of the students, who are therefore able to work in different centres, and professors who can enrich the different universities with their different perspectives. The necessity of such transformation is the consequence of the multilevel interaction of different legal orders within the process of European integration, which furthermore is leading to the development of new mainstream principles (see Chapter 11 by Policastro and Freixes). The new standards of legal education also require new forms of interaction between research and didactic, in a way to enhance the motivation of the students to participate in new activities having scientific and practical relevance, and the professors to develop research teams with direct contact with the students and with the colleagues (see Chapter 12 by Policastro and Castorina). An important element of the legal education and training, is the development of competence to work in bigger teams, where different skills may potentiate. The possibility to extend an electronic platform designed to permit the communication between the enterprises and the university, to develop case studies from the real world of affairs for legal education, poses the problem of joining different training and developing teams, which are in the condition to go beyond the limits of the individual disciplines (see Chapter 13 by Nermend, Piwowarski and Policastro). Indeed, the development of the technological society creates new challenges, which call for a wider interdisciplinary education. An important question concerns how to adapt the curriculum of studies to such needs. The need to create a mental attitude to work and to deal with different professional profiles directs us to take into account an issue such as artificial intelligence, which has a clear application-based framework addressed to join knowledge, skills and competences also with respect to legal education (see Chapter 14 by Policastro, Wąsikowska and Wawrzyniak).[6] Therefore an application of artificial intelligence has been presented, showing that the demand of legal training may occur at the crossroads between different scientific and technological approaches, such as pharmacology and telemedicine. Such an attempt shows a very significant application, in an important public service, which is related to the prevention of the circulation of new psychoactive substances (see Chapter 15 by Bogusławski, Corazza, and Policastro). In this sense the technological society creates new demands for legal training, which appear related to basic services widespread on the territory. Therefore, the demand of evolution of the curricula also needs a growing awareness of the importance to experiment.

As we have said, we have tried to present all these in the hope that they may support a constructive development of different activities, in a way to continue broadening the initiatives, which were inspired and have been developed through the dissemination of the project

6 *See* the journal *Artificial Intelligence and Law*, which appears to be knowledge oriented.

'Menu for Justice – Toward a European Curriculum Studiorum on Judicial Studies'. We would like to thank all the persons and institutions that have been supporting us in this process of dissemination – the participants to the project and the colleagues and friends of the Steering Committee of 'Menu for Justice', the lecturers at the 'European Master in Law and Policies of European Integration: European Constitutional Law and Multilevel Constitutionalism', the Faculty and University colleagues, as well as the Members of the Lawyers' Associations who devoted their time and interest to the development of our debates on innovation in legal education. For want of space, it would be difficult to mention them all: I would mention here only Professor Oscar Garavello, who specially contributed to our interdisciplinary reflection on law and economics, and advocate Michele Di Gianni, who for many years proposed transnational cooperation among lawyers, also by means of press. For editorial reasons we did not have space to include all the materials that we produced, and therefore I hope we may find other possibilities to continue the reflections started somewhere else. Heartfelt thanks to my staff of Szczecin University, as well of the University of Coimbra, for the support in the process of dissemination.

This book, both from the perspective and from the context in which it was developed, has been an opportunity to reflect on who may be the lawyer of tomorrow. Coming back to the reflection with which we started this introduction, I may add that the transformations, which started in Europe and extended worldwide after the end of the 1980s, have been deeply affecting the profession of the lawyer. We experience a growing interaction between different cultures, societies, personal situations, legal, political and economic orders, and this demands the lawyer to search for mediation, taking into account the need to protect the different existential manifestations of the person in the context of interdependence. Especially in the case when the interactions between legal orders make it difficult to understand 'what is the law of the case' (*quid ius*), a satisfactory answer concerning 'what shall be the law' (*quid iuris*)[7] may be given from lawyers who are willing and able to

7 G. Capograssi, 'Il "quid ius" e il "quid iuris" in una recente sentenza', *in Opere di Giuseppe Capograssi*, Tom V, Milano, 1959, pp. 21-26. The author commented a legal decision on the aftermath of World War II, given in a place, Trieste, where the end of hostilities went together with far-reaching partisan activities from different sides. The events took place in 1945. The facts: three former members of railway militia were chaotically accused of having stolen a pig. They were then pushed in a tavern, condemned by a rioting group, brought out naked, assassinated and their bodies were thrown into a foiba hole. However, some of the assassins have been caught and brought to court. Their defense claimed that in that exceptional time people believed it was their right, as veritable sovereigns, to condemn those who were guilty. The judge agreed that such understanding was common in certain environments, but concluded that the alleged behaviour was illegal and that the accused were responsible. The judge claimed that the evidence of such illegality had to be found in sentiment "most alive and ingrained in the peoples' mind, which excluded any possibility to justify the behavior of the accused", and that "there cannot be killed individuals deprived of any possibility of defending themselves and for a guilt enormously disproportioned to the penalty", p. 21. The author of the comment stresses that in any school of law these two realities shall always be present: "the tavern-cavern", on the one hand, and "the court" on the other: "that very little is needed to precipitate the court into a cavern" (p. 26).

overarch the different situations within a coherent[8] construction. The individual efforts of the students and of the lawyers, the efforts of the universities and of the polities develop growingly wide common spaces of higher education, starting from the European Union, are undoubtably important. What makes the difference is how we remain, in the process of learning, focused on outcomes and open to seek and find the values which guarantee the best protection of the human person, thus legitimating law and opening to peaceful and mutually satisfactory arrangements. This shall be the aim of the legal studies, and this requires not only knowledge, but developing skills and competences required to solve new, complex, unpredictable problems by means of law, which is called to guarantee the dignity of human person. For this reason, I would like to dedicate this book to our students, for the enthusiasm and dedication with which they pursue their professional life because of their training.

Pasquale Policastro

Szczecin, Barcelona, Milano, Montpellier,
2 February 2013

8 Aleksander Peczenik, *On Law and Reason*, Dordrecht, 1989, especially pp. 158-211.

Part I
Legal Transformations and Innovation

1 Judicial Activism and Legal Education

Bogusław Banaszak

1.1 The Notion of Judicial Activism

The political and legislative changes in the democratic states in the 20th and 21st centuries were accompanied by the so-called judicial activism, associated, first of all, with the activities of constitutional courts (there where they exist) and supreme courts. It is usually understood as settling the consequences of an ambivalent constitutional norm, as a result of considering the argumentation and choosing the best decision in regard to its effects,[1] in particular when the judgement leads eventually to imposing particular duties on the institutions of the State, increasing or reducing individual rights and freedoms or, in an extreme case, a complete negation of the freedom of legislation in a given area.

1.2 Concerns About the Rise of the Importance of the Courts

It should be added that the rise of the importance of the judicature started already at the beginnings of the liberal democratic state.

> Jefferson had misgivings about too broad a range of power of the Supreme Court. In 1821 he wrote that the Supreme Court secures the rule of the oligarchy and its composure has nothing to do with the will of the nation.[2]

This attitude has remained current until today. The American professor W.J. Quirk, a co-author of a book entitled *Judicial Dictatorship*, stated, "Nowadays it is the courts and not the people that bring about changes in the American society."[3] He has been joined by other scholars and writers – for example, P.J. Buchanan writes,

> We live under the supremacy of judges, whom the Congress tries to oppose. [. . .] This is a real coup d'état. [. . .] In America the majority does not rule. It is a minority that rules, whose visions of what America should be are

1 *See* L. Morawski, *Główne problemy współczesnej filozofii prawa. Prawo w toku przemian*, Warszawa, 2005, p. 22.
2 L. Pastusiak, *Prezydenci*, Vol. I, Warszawa 1989, p. 134.
3 W.J. Quirk & R. Randall Bridwell, *Judicial Dictatorship*, New Brunswick, NJ, 1995, p. vii.

> supported by five judges of the Supreme Court (the majority of the Supreme Court, adn. BB) whose names are not even known to most Americans.[4]

In Europe, some well-known constitutionalists (*e.g.* Hans Klecatsky, Rene Marcic[5]) also expressed their concerns. With some exaggeration, they spoke of the transformation of a law-based state into a judge-based state, and the rule of law into the rule of the judges. "R. Dahrendorf spoke of the epoch [. . .] where the judges assume the function of super-politicians dealing not only with politics but also with ethics."[6]

Similar observations, based on pursuing the changes in the functioning of the public powers and observable shifts of the centres of public decisions, have also been formulated by legal scholars and political scientists. A representative instance of this is the widely quoted formulation by E.W. Böckenförde, who called Germany a "jurisdictional state governed by a constitutional court" (*verfassungsgerichtlichen Jurisdiktionsstaat*),[7] or a statement by B. Schünemann about "a covert change of the constitution from the Bonn democracy to the aristocracy of Karlsruhe".[8] These opinions have been shared by important politicians. By means of an example, I would like to quote Chancellor Konrad Adenauer, who, as long back as in the 1950s of the 20th century, regarded the Constitutional Court as a factor in the political struggle, called it 'the factual dictator of Germany' and said ironically, "Above the Federal Constitutional Court, there is only God Almighty".[9]

Similar voices also appear in Polish political journalism. An example of this is the following statement by S. Janecki:

> The election for the Parliament does not make any sense. In fact, the citizens are not being ruled by the Parliament, nor the government it appoints. It is the judges who rule. This means that the greatest impact upon our lives is exerted by people whom we do not elect, as they in fact elect each other. And they control each other. A judge can not only deprive us of our freedom, destroy the achievements of our life (sometimes of many generations), and block us from working in our profession or taking care of our children. It can tell us what to say in a public debate (there are many weird verdicts on slander).

4 P.J. Buchanan, *Śmierć zachodu*, Wrocław, 2006, p. 218.
5 P. Pernthalter, '*Amplius* on the subject', *in Allgemeine Staatslehre und Verfassungslehre*, Vienna, 1986, p. 249.
6 S. Janecki, 'Oligarchia sędziów', *Wprost* 4 October 2009, p. 5.
7 E.W. Böckenförde, *Staat – Verfassung – Demokratie*, 1992, p. 190.
8 Quote from: H.H. Klein, Gedanken . . ., p. 1143.
9 D. Janicka, *Ustawa Zasadnicza w praktyce Republiki Federalnej Niemiec (1949-1989)*, Toruń, 2009, pp. 247-248.

> It can stigmatize our moral choices [. . .] This state of affairs should arouse dismay, because it is a soft introduction of something like judicial totalitarian rule. As a matter of fact, it is no longer a parliamentary democracy we are dealing with. It is a court oligarchy.[10]

1.3 CONCERNS ABOUT CONSTITUTIONAL COURTS

The concerns about the constitutional courts are intensified by their ability to proclaim void the acts of the democratically elected parliament, expressing the will of the majority of the sovereign subject. This causes controversies in the legal science. Some authors point out that the Constitutional Court misses the democratic legitimation comparable to the legitimation of the legislative, and the fact that in its jurisdiction it attributes its own system of values to the Constitution, just to become its guardian in the next step.[11]

This may result in the Constitutional Court assuming the central, supreme position in the State[12] and turning into not as much a 'negative lawmaker',[13] as a 'substitute lawmaker', because its judgements contain very precise instructions regarding the concord between legislation and the Constitution.[14] Some voices point out that the constitutional jurisdiction is becoming more and more political, which is unavoidable in this situation.[15]

1.4 CRITICISM OF THE ACTIVITY OF THE JUDICATURE

These and similar voices reflect the public criticism of the activities of the judicature. The criticism occurs with diverse intensity in various democratic states. This corresponds to the following statement by L. Morawski:

> One can assume that all control instruments will be effective only if the constitutional courts are willing to submit to them. We cannot however count on this unless there is a public debate which exposes the courts to a strict

10 Janecki 2009.

11 *See, e.g.* A. Podlech, 'Verfassungsgerichtsbarkeit als Grundrechtschutz', *in* H.J. Vogel, H. Simon & A. Podlech (Eds.), *Die Freiheit des Anderen. Festschrift für Martin Hirsch*, Baden-Baden, 1981, pp. 440-444.

12 *See, e.g.* K.A. Bettermann, *Hypotrophie der Grundrechte*, Hamburg, 1984, s. 13.

13 E. Melichar, *Verfassungsgerichtshof und Legislative (w:) Dimensionen des Rechts. Gedächnitsschrift Marcic*, Vienna, 1974, p. 556.

14 A. v. Brünneck, *Verfassungsgerichtsbarkeit in den westlichen Demokratien*, Baden-Baden, 1992, p. 168.

15 *See* Z. Kędzia, *Burżuazyjna koncepcja praw człowieka*, Ossolineum, 1980, p. 334.

> judgement of the public by means of the available mass media. This judgement is needed just because the tribunals are independent and cannot principally be submitted to any external control instruments. In this respect, however, the situation does not look good. Here, again, I would like to quote W. Sadurski. He is certainly right, and he is not alone with his opinion, when he states that in Europe, and in particular in Middle-Eastern Europe, constitutional tribunals enjoy an almost idolatrous authority, and every attempt to criticize them is treated almost like an assassination attempt on the constitutional foundations of the state. [...] This is an awkward situation, when we compare it with the very principal and sometimes extremely critical debates about jurisdiction by the Supreme Court in the USA or Canada. But first of all this situation is very dangerous, because this means that one of the central institutions of the state acts without any control. The strict public evaluation of the jurisdiction by the constitutional court within a free and unrestricted public debate should become such a control tool. We owe the society such a criticism of the Tribunal's decisions, when we think that it does not decide in accordance with the imperatives of constitutional policies. We owe such criticism to the Tribunal itself, too, so that its decisions become as good as possible; and its members should realise that their role in the society is too important to be passed over in silence in the name of respect for the Tribunal's dignity and prestige.[16]

1.5 The Opinions of the Supporters of the Increased Significance of the Judicature

The opinions of supporters of the increased significance of the judicature are typified in the following statement by W. Geiger from the year 1949, just after the German Constitution came into force:

> The Constitution gives supremacy to the Federal Constitutional Court. It occupies the central position in our system, which a parliamentary democracy gives to the parliament, and a presidential democracy to the president. We have got democracy based on the division of powers, in which there dominates the third power in the shape of the Federal Constitutional Court.[17]

16 L. Morawski, 'Zasada trójpodziału władzy. Trybunał Konstytucyjny i aktywizm sędziowski', *Przegląd Sejmowy*, Vol. 4, 2009, p. 45.

17 Quote from: T. v. Danwitz, 'Qualifizierte Mehrheiten für normverwerfende Entscheidungen des BVerfGE ?', *Juristen Zeitung*, Vol. 10, 1996, p. 482.

In this approach

> the constitutional jurisdiction serves the implementation of the primacy of the constitution, which also restricts the power of the Parliament, just as the administrative jurisdiction controls the consistency between what is being done and the acts passed by the executive.[18]

According to the approach corresponding to these statements, the judge should not only apply the law but also make it. It has been pointed out that

> at almost all stages of law making – constitution and bill legislation, law making by the executive branch, and law making by court jurisdiction – there exists a relation between applying the law and lawmaking [. . .] thanks to which it is possible to overcome the mechanisms of subsumption based on the works of Montesque and Laband. In the latter, the judge only carries out the will of the legislator and has no range of freedom in decision making. Contrary to this, due partly but not only to the limited capability of norm makers to predict the future, the normative system is by necessity open and requires a concretization.[19]

In carrying out this concretization, just like the Parliament or other lawmaking institutions, the judge of a constitutional court must take various factors into account, including factors outside the legal sphere that determine the implementation of legal norms, for example, social and economic ones.[20] The range of freedom of the Constitutional Court in taking them into account is much broader than it is in the case of other courts that are obliged to follow not only the Constitution but also other legislations. In this situation, excessive judicial restraint of the Constitutional Court would as a matter of fact lead to a refusal to protect the law.

However, excessive petrification of its jurisdiction and lack of changes would imply that the Constitution will not be developed any longer and will not be able to serve as a foundation of the law in the changing social reality. This idea has also been articulated by the German Federal Constitutional Court in the justification of one of its decisions; it was observed that its task is not lawmaking but finding legal principles in the Constitution.

---

18 D. Merten, 'Demokratischer Recthtsstaat unf Verfassungsgerichtbarkeit', *Deutscher Verwaltungsblatt* 1980, p. 777.

19 N. Achterberg, 'Bundesverfassungsgericht und Zurückhaltungsgebote', *Die Öffentliche Verwaltunng*, Vol. 18, 1977, p. 650.

20 *See* BVerfGE 1, pp. 144-145.

1.6 The Impact of the Judicial Activism on the Legal Education

The lack of a consolidated attitude towards judicial activism in legal sciences has an impact upon legal education. In lectures and other forms of teaching, two different approaches occur – either not mentioning the issue at all or discussing it in a critical or appreciative manner. The preparation of the lawyer for judicial activism is most visible in the case-based method of teaching law. Obviously, it is being preferred in case law countries. However, it is also growing popular in the continental Europe, and there is hardly any country where it is not present to some degree. However, to prepare lawyers for decision-making, there is also a need of information and a critical approach. Therefore the traditional forms of education, and lectures in particular, can be very important to acquire the abilities to work as a judge, who is able to make use of the refined methods needed to comply with the tasks of his profession. First, the sum of theoretical knowledge that is presented in the lectures allows the students to evaluate judicial activism on their own. Second, an active judge needs to draw on the legacy of legal sciences to account for the views presented in the decisions of the cases, even if the views supported by the judge do not currently find general acceptance. This is especially important when the judge deals with a political situation which is not keen towards fundamental values, such as human rights and democracy. The wider the knowledge attained during the studies, the greater the chance that the judge will make use of it during his or her professional career, boldly challenging legal authorities. For this reason, the development in the legal studies of theoretical knowledge, skills to implement such knowledge and capacity to deal with problems arising in complex situations, such as complying with 'The Framework for Qualifications of the European Higher Education Area', appears to be an important call for the universities and the training centres in the direction of a wider implementation of the founding values of European integration.

2 The Evolution of European Constitutional Law and the Training of the Trainers: the Regensburg Conferences

Rainer Arnold

Constitutional law is a legal basis of a State and sets up the institutional structures and the value system of a society. Traditionally, constitutional law has been presented in academic teaching in a preponderantly national view. The today's perspective is quite different; constitutional law in Europe is composed of legal norms stemming from three normative levels which are autonomous but nevertheless interdependent and to a certain extent also interactive: national constitutional law, the basic provisions of the European Union law and the European Convention of Human Rights.[1]

National constitutional law of the 27 Member States of the European Union is significantly influenced by EU law, which has primacy over national law and, in the view of the European Court of Justice as well as of most of the Member States constitutional courts, also over national constitutional law. However, primacy over national constitutional law is not accepted by national constitutional courts insofar as it would override the nucleus of the Constitution, its constitutional identity.[2]

Furthermore, the constitutional law of the 47 Council of Europe Member States (including all the EU members) is largely influenced by the jurisprudence of the European Court of Human Rights, so that a clear convergence tendency in the field of fundamental rights in Europe can be stated. The interdependence of the three constitutional levels in Europe is the basis for the new perspective of constitutional law teaching. It cannot be limited to an isolated analysis and evaluation of the national order but has to consider the three levels as a unity. This unity is not only given within the legal order of the State but also outside

1 *See* R. Arnold, 'The Different Levels of Constitutional Law in Europe and Their Interdependence', *in* J. Nergelius, P. Policastro & K. Urata (Eds.), *Challenges of Multi-Level Constitutionalism*, 21st IVR World Congress, Lund, August 2003, Cracov, 2004, pp. 101-113.

2 *See* R. Arnold, 'Verfassungsidentität und Europäische Integration. Die Perspektive der mittel- und osteuropäischen Verfassungsgerichte', *in* H. Küpper, *Von Kontinuitäten und Brüchen: Ostrecht im Wandel der Zeiten, Festschrift für Friedrich-Christian Schroeder zum 75. Geburtstag*, Frankfurt am Main, 2011, pp. 309-319.

the States in Europe, including the mentioned three orders. Constitutional law in Europe is necessarily *European constitutional law*. This is true not only for the field of values, the fundamental rights and the institutional values as rule of law and democracy but also for the institutional provisions of the Constitution which reflect values and are based on them. State institutions must be seen in the perspective of their functions which serve to attain and maintain democracy, rule of law, 'open statehood'[3] as the principle of friendliness towards the international community, social state orientation and so on.

Given the present *transnational character of constitutional law*, the methodology of research and teaching of this matter must also be transnational, and in our continent 'Europeanized'. EU law can only be understood by means of interpretation principles specifically developed for a supranational body of norms. Also the European Convention of Human Rights cannot be implemented under a bare national perspective. It must be interpreted and applied with the help of the principle of the *effet utile*,[4] which is related to a far-reaching recognition of human rights as European values laid down in the Convention conceived as a living instrument. This comprehensive 'European method' influences also the understanding of the internal constitutional law, which has to apply the same basic principles as they are found in the larger European perspective.

A further consequence of this reflection is that the transnational understanding of constitutional law in the research and academic teaching involves necessarily an *interdisciplinary approach* to it. The historical context, the sociological circumstances, the multilingual basis of the norms stemming from European legal instruments and the philosophical and ethical orientations of the different societies have to be adequately considered when teaching constitutional law in the European integration process.

This context considerably influences the methods of research and of training of the academic teachers. They have necessarily to take into account the European dimension of constitutional law, and have to be aware of the *dynamic developments* of the said three interactive levels of constitutional law. Indeed, such a *'plurilevel' structure* of European constitutional law reinforces this dynamism. Constitutional jurisprudence is the most important indicator of the interaction between such legal levels, which are making the living constitutional law situation in a country. Indeed, formal constitutional reforms are closely linked to those political compromises, which are often necessary for ensuring a qualified

3 *See* 'Offene Staatlichkeit: Deutschland', *in* A. von Bogdandy, P. Cruz Villalón & P.M. Huber (Hrsg.), *Handbuch Ius Publicum Europaeum, Bd. 2:Offene Staatlichkeit – Wissenschaft vom Verfassungsrecht*, Heidelberg, 2008, pp. 3-35.

4 *See* J. Frowein & W. Peukert, *Europäische Menschenrechtskonvention* (3rd ed.), 2009, Einführung (introduction), Rn. 8 with reference to the Airey case, Sér. A 32, 12, Z. 24.

majority in Parliament. In other cases, a referendum is foreseen in the reform process, supported by a public debate sufficient to convince people of the opportunity of a new constitutional solution. However, the dynamic adaptation of the constitutional text to the ongoing social changes takes place through jurisprudence.

Constitution, as the basic legal order of a society, shall bind and work, for an indeterminate time, as the normative orientation for state institutions and the actors in the society. Therefore, each Constitution contains implicitly the invitation to the judges, and specifically to those judges in charge of constitutional interpretation, to carry out this adaptation of the constitutional text. This is according to the perspective that the Constitution is, as we already mentioned, a *living instrument*.

Currently in Europe many constitutions establish a constitutional court in the sense of the Austrian-European type of constitutional justice. This takes place in particular in Central and Eastern Europe. When we have a constitutional court of the said type, the constitutional provisions on the jurisdiction attributed to these courts provide an *explicit* invitation addressed to the constitutional judges, which may be seen even as a normative order to them to fulfil the above-mentioned adaptation task. The problem where the limits for such a judge-made adaptation are to be found is serious, but cannot be elaborated in this contribution. Anyway, an adequate self-restraint of the constitutional courts can avoid conflicts between a legitimate judicial activism and a necessary formal reform of the Constitution.

The importance of constitutional jurisprudence cannot be underestimated, even in legal orders, which do not acknowledge constitutional precedents. Constitutional jurisprudence enjoys generally a high reputation and often has a significant force of conciliating the society in highly disputed matters of ethical and emotional nature. While the moment of the adoption of a formal constitution is static, the application of the Constitution is a long-lasting process with an inherent dynamism. Constitution-making is a basic democratic event, while legislation is a specific democratic process. The general will of the people is expressed by the Constitution, while the specific will of the people is formulated by the legislator. This specific will must conform to the general will, as laid down by the Constitution.[5] Legislation transforms politics into law. Both areas, Constitution and legislation, are complementary areas, not conflicting ones. The competence of the legislator ends where the Constitution begins. However, the legislator implements the Constitution

5 The classic dictum of the Conseil constitutionnel in the case Nouvelle-Calédonie (Déc. No. 85 – 197 du 23 aout 1985, Rec., p. 70) characterizes the new approach of constitutionality of legislation as a basic requirement of the modern rule of law concept: legislation expresses the general will only if it conforms to the Constitution ("la loi n'exprime la volonté générale que dans le respect de la Constitution").

and has, therefore, a certain impact on its contents. Functionally, Constitution and legislation are linked. Rule of law in the modern sense means supremacy of the Constitution, constitutionality of legislation and primacy of legislation over executive and jurisprudential action.

The most significant phase of modern constitutionalism in Europe has been the transformation process of former communist countries. In view of making the new legal principles efficiently prevail over national politics, constitutional courts of the Austrian-European type[6] have been established in Central, Eastern and South-Eastern Europe (with the exception of Estonia), which have been seen as important guarantees for the new approach. Constitutional jurisprudence has therefore obtained a primary rank in the transformation process. The constitutional courts have not revealed to be political actors but vigilant observers and re-actors when this process was threatened. The orientation of these courts has to be qualified as clearly modern, taking up well-established democratic and pluralistic concepts from 'old' Europe and developing them further in a positive sense, even beyond the standards in some traditional Western countries.[7]

Today's pluri-level constitutionalism in its dynamic, advanced form requires new approaches in research and academic teaching. It seems to be of importance to create a transnational reflection and debate forum as it has been the case with fourteen International Congresses on European and Comparative Constitutional Law organized annually at the University of Regensburg, by the author of this article. Establishing a network in this sense means to broaden the intellectual basis of constitutional law reflections by the intensive and immediate exchange of perspectives stemming from different legal cultures and diverging historical experiences in law practice. Legal approximation in an area of intended integration must try to find its sources in the variety of legal thinking. Common cultural links can be found in the European Union law and, in the fields of values, in particular in the European Convention of Human Rights which have convergence effects but are also influenced themselves by the variety of legal cultures in Europe. Diversity and unity are not contradictions but complementary phenomena which have a mutual fertilizing impact. As basic law concepts are primary cultural factors, European legal culture is emerging but can only be consolidated by the respect of diversity. Subsidiarity also in the field of values[8] is therefore indispensable for the survival of the upcoming European legal culture.

---

6 *See* Th. Öhlinger, 'Die Entstehung und Entfaltung des österreichischen Modells der Verfassungsgerichtsbarkeit', *in* L.K. Adamovich, *Festschrift für Ludwig Adamovich zum 70. Geburtstag*, 2002, pp. 581-600.

7 *See* R. Arnold, 'Constitutional Courts of Central and Eastern European countries as a dynamic source of modern legal ideas', *in Tulane European & Civil Law Forum*, Bd. 18, New Orleans, LA, 2003, pp. 99-115.

8 *See* Paolo G. Carozza, 'Subsidiarity as a Structural Principle of International Human Rights Law', 97 *AJIL* 2003, pp. 38-79.

Perception of legal ideas seems to be possible only in a *process of discourse*. This discourse must be necessarily transnational, going beyond the political frontiers in Europe, referring to the wide area of the leading Council of Europe concepts of the basic values of the modern democratic and anthropocentric society. The discourse must furthermore be *universal* for avoiding a potentially limited perspective. Values are globalizing and require universal respect, in full awareness of divergences resulting from different identities in law, politics and culture. The core elements of human and institutional values are to be considered as universally binding, being an indispensable fundament for all human beings and the international community. The impact of the Regensburg network will be seen in the years. However, in organizing and developing it we tried to create a forum of discussion, stressing the equal and fundamental importance of all the participants. This dialogue process became not only a moment of connection and dialogue between experts but also a forum permitting the dialogue on how to understand and to transmit the values of the constitutional integration. It became therefore a moment of network-based training of the trainers, in which everybody was a trainer and trainee at the same time.

In our opinion constitutional law research and teaching should be based on these methods. Indeed, networking has a growing importance for complying with the legal needs of modern, anthropocentric societies.

3 Compliance: Challenge or Chance for Legal Education?

Bartosz Makowicz

The issue of compliance in companies has in recent years significantly become more important in Germany and Europe and has indirectly affected various economic and social processes. This article outlines the fundaments of the scientific nature of the compliance topic and asks whether and how legal education in Europe might contribute in this context.

3.1 Introduction

The object of academic research is pursued with any activity that by form and content is considered to be a scheduled attempt to determine the truth. The results obtained in this way are passed on by teaching; thus, the two functions of a university and – through this institution – of legal education are being defined. By this process, new fields of research are being developed and practically implemented into everyday life.

While in recent years several new areas of academic research have been established, science was less concerned with the development of a holistic and forward-looking approach for companies, which would make these entities more resistant to irregularities, like corruption, antitrust or even unethical behaviour. Even big business scandals in recent years were not reason enough for science to look out for such a conception. The private business sector, however, seems to have found a solution on their own: it is called compliance.

The chapter aims to provide evidence that compliance forms a new field for academic research, which is – as an interdisciplinary subject – rooted in many conventional disciplines and should therefore be included in their research activities. The findings of compliance research shall be transferred into practice by teaching.[1] Given the fact that most of the people in business practice who are responsible for compliance (the so-called Chief Compliance Officer) are lawyers by education, it is the responsibility of legal education to include at least some aspects of this broad interdisciplinary matter in its curricula. Therefore, when dealing with modernization of legal education, we should consider the topic of compliance.

1 Interested persons are invited to join the Center for Compliance Research (CCR), which is being established at the European University Viadrina. For more information, please contact: ppl@europa-uni.de.

3.2 A Multidisciplinary Perspective

What stands basically behind 'this' compliance? The most common definition of the term seems to be moderate: the fulfilment of a rule, be it legal or ethical, by the company as a whole. Thus the definition includes an approach for legal education: primarily, compliance shall prevent, clarify and clear violations of the law.

Although the definition mentioned above is very useful for the general understanding of compliance, a more distinguished one is needed in view of the multiple functions of compliance. In searching for an appropriate definition, a holistic approach should be pursued to meet the objectives of compliance. Thus, 'compliance' could be described as a flexible system of thoughtfully complied measures, respecting the principle of proportionality, which – taken as a whole – provide for prevention, detection and rehabilitation of irregularities in the company and its business relations to create a sustainable shareholder value and a risk-free environment for business operations. This poses the question: how to identify such risky areas and how to set up such a complicated system? Right there lies the rub! Without looking beyond a discipline, it would not be possible to set up a compliance system. By this, allegations of the compliance sceptics can be rejected: Although the order of compliance is not something new, something unprecedented is its method of implementation – the holistic concept, which is subsumed under the key word of compliance and spread across several disciplines. These disciplines shall be mentioned here exemplarily, as they could be included into the legal curriculum at least as optional courses to allow the acquisition of additional skills, which might also enhance the understanding of the law in general.

3.3 Law

The reluctance of some lawyers towards the topic of compliance may derive from the fact that this subject cannot be forced into one specific field of law and thus is interdisciplinary within the law itself. Let us have a closer look on the typical legal fields like private, public and criminal law.

The ambiguity of the labour law compliance may serve as an example in private law. While, on the one hand, it is about complying with labour laws, on the other, both individual and collective labour laws form part of the instruments with which a compliance system might be implemented in the company. Other compliance-relevant areas in the sphere of the private law are taken from corporate-, commercial-, contract- or company laws and many more. An equally broad base for compliance can be observed in the field of public law.

Not only the regulation of the credit system – which has increased significantly during the financial crisis – but the highly regulated pharmaceutical industry or the insurance industry may serve here as ideal examples. Even during the process of the development of a new product, a compliance officer should be assisting to prevent the introduction of a product that does not fulfil the necessary legal requirements. Furthermore, there may also emerge risks related to public laws compliance. We have in mind taxation laws, building – and environmental laws, or social – and public procurement laws. Finally, the criminal law, and especially the law relating to white-collar crimes, plays a role in the area of compliance, which must not be underestimated. Criminal liability might be very painful and sometimes even surprising, particularly if it derives from extraterritorial regulations which are applicable in other countries, like the recent case of the UK Bribery Act.

It should be the task of legal education to motivate law students to look beyond their own nose – here, to look beyond a certain field of law – and to explain the existing 'interfaces', and namely, the relations with other legal issues. How does state control law affect the formation of civil law, and which values are embodied in the constitutions that have to be protected in criminal law? As a result, a trained lawyer will understand much better the different legal perspectives, out of which a single object – a specific company – can be observed.

3.4 ECONOMICS

While the legislator provides for a catalogue of legislation that for a single company is hard to overlook but necessary to observe, business studies equip the companies with a number of methods to implement such compliance systems. Thus, for example, an appropriate risk management system forms the basis of any compliance system. Potential events shall be identified and classified, possible actions shall be documented and responses shall be designed. This also takes into account the aforementioned flexibility – ready-made solutions do not exist. Instead, when it comes to creating appropriate structures, a minimalist approach regarding the principle of proportionality should be adopted. The microeconomic analysis of compliance and therefore the understanding of the functioning of the company are essential for good compliance. The compliance officer should – just like a tailor – first identify the needs of the company in order to design the suit (the compliance system) later. There are reports of negative examples everywhere around. Too rigid compliance structures lead, for example, in many companies, to conflict situations with the distribution section. Sound knowledge of business economics is therefore essential to create a compliance system; nobody wants to wear a suit that does not fit. These processes should be accompanied by business informatics (IT-based compliance).

Not less important is the function of compliance for the national economy. This is exemplified by a simple causal relationship: the more companies introduce compliance structures, the fewer violations are committed. This in turn will generate a number of positive economic effects: first, the economy as a whole is considered to maintain a proper culture of compliance, which provides for more transparency and, in turn, for increased trust of investors and trading partners. Furthermore, the state budget will have to lose less due to machinations. The market will be strengthened through transparent structures and with it the overall economy and prosperity.

3.5 Other Social Sciences

A well-functioning compliance system is further also considered to be a communication system. What is meant here is the individual- and mass communication, *i.e.* the areas of media- and communication studies. Good business communication is crucial to the success or failure of the compliance system. Good compliance not only starts with the fact that the management is committed to the assumed values and acts accordingly (*voice from the top*). It shall equally start with the individual employees (*voice from the bottom*). Appropriate training and additional measures affect the behaviour of the employees and their moral concepts and contribute to the compliance successes by awareness building. With the essential knowledge of the art of communication and some skills, even an occurred irregularity can be 'sold' to the public as a compliance success: the irregularity is detected thanks to compliance methods. There are currently reprocessing activities, etc. Those messages reach us via the mass media.

Directly linked to good corporate communication is the psychological component of compliance. Thus, for example, the behavioural psychology, which deals with the study of nonverbal communication, *i.e.* the so-called body language, will provide essential insights for the detection measures. Whether internal or external – investigators are confronted with the respondents and must be able to 'read' their behaviour. A good compliance officer is furthermore in constant contact with the different corporate layers and with the outside world. Not only in conversation with the Board or the sales manager but also in interaction with the outside – be it with the prosecutor or the fiscal authorities – in all these cases, soft skills are of essential importance.

3.6 Philosophy

A severe loss of reputation and a corresponding loss of revenue are not necessarily rooted in a violation of the law. An irregularity in the meaning of compliance may also derive from an immoral and unethical behaviour. Generally accepted values have to be observed – also in the business. As once the business ethicist Peter Ulrich wrote, it is necessary to clarify the questionable relationship between the economic intrinsic logic and ethical sanity and to determine it in a sustainable and life-supporting way. However, how should it be implemented? Here compliance could provide the answer. Of use could also be a quote of the former head of the Shell Group, Sir Geoffrey Chandler, who said that "[. . .] Doing right because it is right needs to be the foundation of business". Here science should provide for practical concepts of implementation of a value-based compliance.

3.7 Setting of Rules

Where classical law reaches its limits, but where there is a compelling regulatory need for comprehensive compliance, the area of 'rule setting' by the company itself starts. Internal corporate guidelines – known also as code of conduct – have gained importance in recent times not only for the accompanying and supplementary function of their law but also in their structuring role. They also ensure that in the areas with a legal vacuum, concrete countermeasures are at hand. This is true, on the one hand, to protect a whistle-blower or, on the other hand, for defensive reactions of a suspected person accompanying an internal investigation. Also in these areas, more solid research results would provide valuable information. The existing models should be thoroughly scientifically investigated.

Once the code of conduct has been created and adjusted to the particular needs of the company, there is a question of its implementation to make it to a dynamic document. Again at this side, the legal regulations are to be mentioned, since only by legal means a binding power of the code of conduct can be created.

3.8 Conclusion

Compliance provides enough material for further research and teaching in various disciplines and should be integrated into the legal education. This chance should be primarily used by the law, as here lies the emphasis of compliance, namely, in fulfilling the legal regulations. The interdisciplinary character of compliance serves as the best example that, due to the complexity of today's world and the processes occurring in it, combined training and study courses which comprise several subjects form appropriate answers.

In the long run, legal education will not stay unaffected by this development. Here, too, interdisciplinary elements have to be added gradually, so that future lawyers not only understand the law and its application, but are able to follow associated processes and to develop solutions to prevent legal violations. It is time to break with the conventional law courses in favour of a modern multidisciplinary approach. In this respect, it is not about an *either-or* but about an *and*; compliance is an example for the fact that interdisciplinary questions are a challenge *and* a chance for legal education.

4 The First or the Last? On the Deficit of Human Rights Education in Turkey*

İbrahim Ö. Kaboğlu

Human rights have been a historical problem in the development of contemporary politics in Turkey. The insufficient approach to their protection not only has been jeopardizing the possibility of Turkey to obtain a full accession to European Union but is ever since a cause of internal instability. We always find, nevertheless, the government ready to treat lightly the gravity of the data. Lastly, following the report of the European Court of Human Rights (ECtHR) of 2012, Turkey took the second place in the list of the pending cases, with 16,879 files. As on 31 December 2012, only Russia took the first place in this list with 28,593 cases. According to 2012 data of EtCHR, in 123 cases EtCHR concluded its proceedings with decisions against Turkey, with at least one condemnation.

However, to compare the human rights protection in Russia and in Turkey is not a simple task. We have to take into account the demographic factor: Russia has many more inhabitants than Turkey, and so the number of condemnations says very little about the real state of affairs. There is also another important factor at stake: Turkey is a member of the Council of Europe since the beginning (9 August 1949), while Russia adhered to it in 1996.[1]

Notwithstanding these facts, the government did not lose its usual attitude in commenting such news. According to the press release of a EU minister in Turkey, "The authority to report the government is only and only in the hands of our nation". Not contending with the said releases, the Minister continued his speech, saying, "The 'sick man' of yesterday has recovered itself and will find solutions to the sicknesses in Europe [. . .]". Furthermore, it was added that, "[t]he foreseen reforms will be formed considering the European Convention of Human Rights (ECHR), EU acquits and the case laws of EtCHR until 2013, likewise the previous practices" (2012 Report of Ankara).

Before going into brief considerations on the consistency of these reforms, I would like to pose two preliminary questions concerning the present state of affairs. The first is whether

* İ.Ö. Kaboğlu, 'Human Rights Education in Turkey', in M. Dartan & M. Cebeci (Eds.), Human Rights Education and Practice in Turkey in the Process of Candidacy to the EU, Marmara University European Community Institute, İstanbul, 2002, pp. 103-112.

1 İ.Ö. Kaboglu, 'İHAM önündeki Türkiye (birinci mi, sonuncu mu?) /Turquie devant la Cour Européenne des droits de l'Homme (la première ou la dernière?)', *BirGün*, 31 January 2013.

the Turkish government is truly interested to undertake steady progress in the respect for human rights. The attitude towards the accomplishment of EU standards in this field, which specifies this target as far as 2023, poses serious doubts. The second question is whether the steps taken by Ankara in the last months and weeks, as well as the fourth judicial package, which is on the way, may be sufficient for Turkey to catch up with the standards of ECHR.

The statements of the Minister of Justice relating the steps that are made by Ankara brought us to the conclusion that human rights in Turkey are perceived in a quantitative manner more than a question concerning the quality of social, political and legal relations. Here are some factors that we shall take into account: (1) the said attitude procrastinated rather than speeded up the accomplishment of European standards; (2) the fact that legislation is addressed to meet the quantitative issues makes the reforms partial, and never systemic; (3) the behaviour of the Minister of Justice, as if violation of human rights would not be an issue for the legislative power and the executive power; (4) also, the legislative improvements that are discussed still reflect an adverse attitude towards those who infringed law; (5) beyond this, the legal remedies do not so far permit any qualitative restoration of the perpetrated violations.

All these questions and considerations justify, in our opinion, to consider an important problem that is at the bottom of this article. The question of the respect of human rights is always rooted deeply in legal and political education. In this regard, we see quite an insufficient inclusion of human rights in legal, political and administrative sciences in Turkey, which do not seem to be based on taking human rights as their foundation. Therefore, our question is: which innovation in legal education may be deemed as supporting the needed transformation in the understanding of human rights?

This question is important both for society and for experts, in Turkey and abroad. Indeed, the insufficient consideration of human rights has simple and very complex manifestations. Among the simple and evident elements, we may show the ones affecting justice, namely, the exams of choosing the judges and the prosecutors held just by the Ministry of Justice. Furthermore, there is the practice to demand a reference from the candidates to such examinations. We believe that it is not only degrading but also unethical of the persons who will dispense justice. Providing a full list of the issues which jeopardize the correct application of human rights and which may be solved through clear and punctual legislative changes goes, however, beyond the purposes of this publication. However, this example clearly shows the need for systemic reforms. We may expose here some of the consequences of such a state of affairs. Indeed, thousands of violations of liberties are done through activities complying with the legislation in force. This often calls for very violent protest, which generates vicious circles. Furthermore, a considerable amount of such violations is based on the practice of 'oppressing the democratic opposition' or coming to terms with the past. These elements confirm the existence of a culture which is fundamentally suspicious towards the rights, and this is confirmed by the resistances of the government to fulfil its international obligations despite the evidence given by the EtCHR.

What we say does not mean that Turkey is not enacting legislation apparently aimed at pursueing compliance with human rights. We have, for example, the recently enacted Law No. 6234 ordering the establishment of a commission to review ongoing cases against Turkey at the ECtHR and offer a remedy in terms of compensation to the plaintiffs.[2] The said commission, comprising five people, may undertake the issue of violations based on the excessive length of proceedings. Complainants who have applied to the ECtHR will be able to apply to the commission within six months of the law coming into effect, and the commission will decide the cases within nine months at the most. There is furthermore the right to petition by individuals to the Constitutional Court. However, since the reforms undertaken in Turkey are not dealing systemically with the problems, they produce effects which are very limited when concerning the quality of human rights.[3]

Trying to give further evidence of the reasons for this situation, we will present some consideration on the activities related to training on human rights, which were performed in the past, and the consequent reactions of political power. Indeed, at the beginning of the 21st century, the strengthening of human rights in Turkey has been carried out by means of complementary activities, which included the adoption of new legislation, the transformation of the institutional structures and issues concerning legal application. Many educational activities were planned to improve human rights practice.

This process has been initiated through the National Committee for Human Rights Education. The Committee was instituted in the frame of the UN's Decade for Human Rights Education.

The National Committee held its first meeting on 3 September 1998. It decided, among other things, to compile an inventory of the human rights education provided in Turkey and the efforts related to these activities. Furthermore, it undertook to determine the educational needs with regard to the human rights problems in Turkey and the main target groups. It also undertook also to develop a strategy of human rights education in Turkey in the long-, medium- and short run.[4]

---

2 Law No. 6234 was adopted in accordance with the judgements of the ECHRs: *Affaire Daneshpayeh v. Turquie*, 16 October 2009; *Ümmühan Kaplan v. Turquie*, 20 March 2012.

3 *See* the debate which appeared on 'Today's Zaman', on 25 January 2013 (by Aydin Albayrak).

4 Human Rights Education Program of Turkey (1998-2007), National Committee of the Decade for Human Rights Educations, July 1999, Ankara, p. 11.

Therefore, it was decided to prepare and implement human rights training programmes that addressed the following target groups: teachers, police officers, district governors and their substitutes, judges and prosecutors and prison officers. The training programme concerning teachers was initiated in 1999. The second programme was concerning governors and substitute governors. It was prepared by the National Committee in collaboration with the Ministry of Internal Affairs. The third programme, which covered the security forces, involved the cooperation of the National Committee for Human Rights Education and the Council of Europe. Furthermore, the training of the police instructors and the police officers was developed also by means of a yearly project entitled 'The Police's Professional Activities and Society' [. . .].
The fourth programme was more complex, since it aimed to contribute to the human rights training of judges and public prosecutors. It was prepared by the National Committee in cooperation with representatives of the Ministry of Justice and of the Council of Europe. It was envisaged that this programme would be conducted between October 2002 and December 2004 and had to cover the whole of Turkey. It involved three-stage activities. In the first stage, five sessions took place in Ankara, Antalya, Diyarbakır, Istanbul and Trabzon. In each session, which lasted five days each, were admitted 40 judges and prosecutors. The main topics considered included European Convention on Human Rights and its implementation.

The second stage was implemented by bringing together the five groups mentioned above: a total of 214 judges and prosecutors participated in this activity. The third stage was realized all over Turkey, in 115 centres of education, and each course involved a group consisting of 50-60 judges and prosecutors. The activities involved a total of 9,308 judges and prosecutors and lasted nearly two years. The ECHR and its implementation were again the main topic of the courses. Each course lasted 30 hours.

The experts chosen as lecturers in these three stages formed units of a mixed character. Most of the experts chosen in the first two stages were European and Turkish academics. In the third stage, most of the experts were Turkish academics, judges and prosecutors.[5]
During the same period, that is, from 2002 to 2004, the Council of Europe and the European Commission (European Union) launched, in collaboration with the Turkish authorities, a joint project aimed at increasing human rights awareness among judges, other public officials and the public at large and at reviewing draft and existing legislation to ensure its conformity with European standards. Turkey's National Committee

5 I. The project to support training education of candidate judges and public prosecutors on human rights; II. The project to support training education of members of supreme courts; III. The project to support training education of 9308 judges and public prosecutors (May 2002-May 2004), Turkish Republic prime ministry, the National Committee of Ten Years of HR Education.

for Human Rights Education played an important role in the accomplishment of this project. Furthermore, the Human Rights Advisory Board carried out several initiatives to increase public awareness on human rights. In this frame, several scholarly events on the European Convention of Human Rights and most notably three symposia sponsored by the country's high courts, helped to increase human rights awareness. They were dedicated to the ECHR and Judicial Power (September 2003), the ECHR and Administrative Jurisdiction (October 2003) and the ECHR and Constitutional Jurisdiction (February 2004).

Moreover, the Ministry of Justice and the Justice Academy of the same ministry provided extensive training on the new criminal legislation pertaining to human rights. Yet, the Academy needs much work to develop into a strong and independent training centre serving all of Turkey's judiciary.

However, the project itself has given results which are only partial, and this poses, once more, the question of how to approach legal training on fundamental rights. Regarding this issue, as I already stressed ten years ago,

> [l]astly, insufficient planning and coordination must be mentioned as a negative factor. To eliminate the latter, all public institutions and non-governmental organizations which prepare and put into practice human rights education programs must act in coordination with the National Committee of Human Rights Education. The difficulty of eliminating the traditional habits of civil servants within the framework of a formation based on a unilateral relationship of office, not based on equality, must also be mentioned. What is even worse is that public bodies which have been organized in a rigid hierarchical structure constantly opt for self-defending reactions instead of making use of self-criticism. Despite all of these factors, all ongoing official and unofficial efforts pertaining to human rights may be evaluated as a serious process of information. The reforms mentioned so far, the activities of institutional development and education are contributing to the reinforcement of the rule of law and to its development. However, they should not make us ignore the need for a substantial change of conception in the field of human rights.[6]

Although the above-mentioned programmes contributed to improve the knowledge and the skills, especially of the judges and the prosecutors, in the field of human rights, their effects were limited due to the reaction of the government, which was full of ambiguities.

6 Kaboğlu 2002, pp. 109-110.

Indeed, at the beginning of 2005, the government limited the activities of the consulting institutions for human rights established at the Prime Minister Office. It preferred to cooperate on the subject with its partisans, getting rid of the specialists of human rights. Programmes for training on human rights lost momentum and consistency. Apart from the political attitude shown by the government in these years, we see that, notwithstanding the efforts to form the judges and the prosecutors, we assist in the decadence of the jurisdictional organs. Indeed they often turn into institutions adding violations of human rights over violations of human rights.

Concerning the solutions to be adopted to the problems, we shall reflect, first of all, on the fact that this general aversion to the training programmes reflects the defensive and ambiguous attitude of the Turkish political power. To overcome this state of affairs and to eradicate such a mentality, which opposes power to rights, we need to accomplish a deep social and political reflection of national and transnational character. Here the role of education and innovative tools, which permit societies to join in a frank political debate within European Union and the Council of Europe, may play a very important role. Trying to underline the priorities to this end, I would mention the following: (1) the government shall decide to promote human rights. Political will and political priorities play a deciding role in these matters; (2) structural reforms are needed, including the independence of the judiciary; (3) the supervision of political authorities on the queries on human rights shall be suppressed; (4) the value of the opinion of the experts in the field of human rights shall be adequately considered; (5) the eduction system, research, legal studies and judicial training shall be founded on a systemic understanding of the human rights. Human rights should not be treated as only one sector of interest, and the reflection on the issue should not be related to casuistic and partial considerations. Respect for human rights shall be conceived, in the process of education, as the foundation of the polity. Here we need innovation in the contents and in the methods, and, in the same understanding, of education and the training process.

Part II
New Approaches, New Doubts

5 Legal Educology as General and Special Science of Education: Lithuanian and Transnational Experiences in the Field of Higher Education

Tomas Berkmanas

In this article we aim to consider the aspect of higher education in law in the perspective of 'educology'.[1] Legal educology thus, as a section of the general field of educology, has to comply with the general frameworks of higher education. However, it is also a unique science of education requiring special approaches to teaching, which are not always coherent with the general models. In this chapter we will linger on some aspects of the configuration of the two modes of legal educology – *i.e.* (1) being part of a general model and (2) being special – and provide with some hints on the directions in which the teaching of lawyers could be developed or where problems could be raised. There are five sections in this chapter posing five relevant questions in a generative way.

5.1 What Should Be the Interaction Between Legal Profession and Higher Legal Education?

The interrelationship between the profession and higher education in the field of law is probably one of the closest in the context of the totality of fields where higher education is conducted. In contrast, many academic domains either do not have direct professional counterparts (as philosophy, history, mathematics), or the development and contents of the academic domain very much dictate the same of the professional domain (as in pedagogy, psychology, etc.). But in the field of law those two processes are, at the very least, much more reciprocal. Indeed, how future lawyers should be taught and develop their skills is considerably influenced by the developments in the legal profession. Very few domains in universities have such a quality.

1 For the application of educology in other fields of knowledge, *see* L. Duobliene, 'Moral Education in Lithuania: An Educology of Teaching. Understanding and Caring versus Teaching Reasoning', *International Journal of Educology*, 2005 Lithuanian Special Issue, p. 1. *See*, for more in general, the website called 'Educology': <www.era-usa.net/contributingpapersset1.html>.

Everyone knows that legal studies are *professional* studies. However, the usual place of the professional studies is not in the universities but in the professional schools. The title of the latter speaks by itself; however, if we should consider separately universities and professional schools, this should mean that the two types of higher education institutions should not cover the same fields. Apart from any consideration based upon European historical traditions, if we were to adopt such a perspective of 'separation' by letting legal education inside their campus, universities should do it at the expense of their being *universities*. In this context it is an interesting linguistic fact in itself that in the United States we have '*schools* of law', while in Europe the usual title of the corresponding higher educational institutions is '*faculty* of law'. Also it is worth noting that in Lithuania the so-called *colleges* (which essentially are professional schools) have the right to conduct basic legal education and provide the professional bachelor degree in law.

Nevertheless, legal education, if not the historical core, is at least a long-lived dweller of the university campus. Why? The ages of the domination of the positivistic doctrine in law have almost erased the understanding, which originally had a key meaning, that the presence of those *schools* inside the university campus is very much beneficial for both universities and schools of professions, which, similar to law, involve prolonged training and a formal qualification. The statement that by being together universities and schools of law enrich each other is therefore not only related to the past, but has a present and real significance. Indeed, it again becomes apparent in the contemporary world where the requirements for a good lawyer are more and more related to *universal* knowledge and creativity, since legal practice may not be related just to its mechanical application.

All this might require rather unique forms of interaction between academic and professional fields. The question that could be posed here is to what extent legal profession should affect the process of higher legal education, having in mind not only the curricula but many other facets as the methodology, length of classes, structure of credits, and so on? Should it reach the level of the full-scale accreditation and the substantial dictation of the rules to the universities on how they should conduct legal studies as it is, for example, with the Bar Association in the United States? European practice is not only to diminish the scale of accreditation but to avoid any of institutionalized influence.[2] Of course, there are other forms of how the legal profession influences higher legal education. For example, legal practitioners may participate in some administrative processes or bodies inside universities or law faculties. Or, in many cases, they teach there and therefore are a part of the teaching staff, thus *de facto* affecting educational processes therein. The question at this point is: is it enough? In the United States the situation is probably the same as in Europe

2 Only the UK makes an exception here, but that is not a surprise considering the proximity of the traditions.

with those other forms of influence; but *besides* that they also have the institutionalized influence. The question whether it is desirable to follow the US example may be left open.

Furthermore, legal education in the United States is famous for being one of the most prestigious in the world, and to catch up with it was one of the policies of the Bologna process. But Bologna process (as a matter of reframing the education) made much more visible impact on the other aspects of higher legal education – related to its inner structure than to its outside influences. Thus we turn to the other question.

5.2 HOW CAN WE JUSTIFY THE *TWO-LEVELS MODEL* OF HIGHER LEGAL EDUCATION?

Under the Bologna model, two levels (or cycles) should be present in higher legal education – first (or undergraduate) and second (or graduate). Before the Bologna process, the integrated model of legal education was dominating in Europe, and this model is still applied in such countries as Germany, Hungary, Italy, Lithuania, etc. Generally, the *two-level approach* to higher legal education is far from being a universal phenomenon. In the United States higher legal education is conducted at a level corresponding to the graduate level in Europe.

Apparently, the separation into two levels posed the problem as that of the undergraduate level. What are the career prospects of the graduate students having only the bachelor's degree in law? This is, however, more a technical than an educological problem, and it may be solved rather easily. For example, in Lithuania a person may practise as an attorney having *only* the bachelor's degree in law; of course, if he wants to be a judge, he must have more than that. However, the educological problem as related to the *structuring* of legal education in levels is mostly related to the graduate level. Why should we separate this smaller part as 'graduate studies' in the overall process of higher legal education? What is the role and place of this 'snapped off' part of this initially coherent process as it is in the integrated or one-level model?

There might be two educological dimensions here: (1) specialization of a lawyer and (2) universalization of a lawyer, the latter relating to the interdisciplinary or non-legal education. These apparently different dimensions are, as a matter of fact, very much interrelated. When you have the specialization process (excluding the specialization just in the field of law), usually at the same time it must be interdisciplinary. For example, to specialize in knowledge and skills in the administrative or international law, you must teach public administration or international relations or some other purely administrative or political study areas. Therefore the configuration of these two dimensions of the development of knowledge and skills is rather symbiotic, and as a symbiotic whole it may provide good grounds to separate it as a distinct – graduate – level of higher legal education.

However, in Lithuania sometimes a concern is expressed that lawyers are too specialized – they know well only the field of their specialization. The specialization of a lawyer, if it is done through the requirement of a separate level of higher legal education, enhances the phenomenon of over-specialization. Therefore, there follows another important question in this regard, which is dealt with separately in the next section.

5.3 To What Extent Are Interdisciplinary Education and Complementary Education in Non-Legal Matters Fit for Higher Legal Education?

We can generally agree that an interdisciplinary approach to knowledge and training is important as such in the overall legal education. Even though legal studies, as we already mentioned, are professional studies, they are still considered to be a part of *university* education. As much as it is the case, this education should provide *universal* scope of expertise and understanding. This thesis is reaffirmed by the necessities related to the contemporary requirements and expectations from the legal profession and, especially, from the judiciary. Judges have to cease pretending being only the 'mouth of law' and start to creatively, morally and responsibly participate in the judicial process. For that they must have a much wider *Weltanschauung* than they presently have. Such wider conception, however, may be obtained only by means of a wide interdisciplinary teaching and an extension of legal education also to non-legal matters.

However, the question is, where should be the place of such kind of extended approach to teaching in higher legal education? There are two general approaches possible: (1) The first and the most common in Europe is the approach where interdisciplinary and non-legal education is conducted more at the subsequent levels of higher legal education, especially at the second level; instead, pure legal professional education is provided at the earlier level of legal training, essentially in undergraduate studies. (2) The second approach could be considered the one where interdisciplinary and non-legal education is conducted more at the initial stages of higher legal education, although not completely lacking at the later stages of education; for example, a substantial or the whole part of undergraduate education could be considered as including interdisciplinary and non-legal subjects, while purely legal professional education is started at the later stages of higher education. This approach is implemented in the United States, although it is not totally absent in Europe. For example, in Lithuania it is implemented in Vytautas Magnus University, where in the integrated studies of first and second levels, the initial stages (especially first two years) are very much focused on the general interdisciplinary or non-legal subjects (as related to the political sciences, history, philosophy, ethics, logics, psychology, languages, etc.). Later on, especially starting from the third year of studies, students are gradually transferred to purely legal professional training, although some interdisciplinary courses may be taught at the very end of studies (fifth year).

It might be stated that the necessities of a wider *Weltanschauung* of a future lawyer should let us give the priority to the second approach. It is because students who learn law should have the basics of this wider perspective, and therefore, in this context, it might be beneficial to make the interdisciplinary approach a continuous facet of legal education.

Furthermore, contemporary processes of globalization and the necessity to transform the future lawyer into a *global* lawyer require universalization of legal education not only in the direction of making nexuses between disciplines but also in the direction of building bridges between legal systems and cultures. Accordingly, curricula of higher legal education have to be continuously enriched by courses having a clearly comparative dimension. Students should be taught not to learn some parts of information by heart but how to use that information and synthesize it crossing different cultural and disciplinary contexts. This leads to the next question.

5.4 What Should Be the Role of the Information-Oriented and the Skills-Oriented Approach to Higher Legal Education in the Contemporary World?

Clearly, information-oriented legal education – dominated by the dictation of the information by a lecturer to the student – is very much outdated in the contemporary world of information. Information today is abundant and easily accessible. About the curricula of legal education today, there is no need to necessarily cover all those masses of information as it was done in more classical forms of legal education where curricula covered very much abundantly the fields of civil law, criminal law, procedural law, constitutional law and so on. Now all laws, statutes, cases and codes are at hand. Therefore information today must be learnt to use and apply through the active participation of students in the learning process. There is no better way to do that than through the Socratic method and case studies – the method which was continuously applied in legal studies in Vytautas Magnus University in Lithuania.

Such transformation presupposes a fundamental reshaping of the curricula and of the methodologies of higher legal education. They should clearly allow condensing the purely legal education, for example, from five years (as it usually is in the model of integrated studies) to three years. This either frees up 'space' for the interdisciplinary education as well as for non-legal subjects in the general curriculum of legal education or, at the very least, allows condensing purely legal education to the equivalent of one level (either graduate or undergraduate) of higher education. In the latter case not only the Bologna model becomes viable, but also the US approach to higher legal education reaffirms its sustainability.

However, in the context of the development of technologies, one other challenge to higher legal education – especially the skills-oriented teaching – emerges. This poses the final question of the chapter.

5.5 How the Distance Learning Technologies Should Affect Legal Studies, Especially the Specific Skills Development Necessities Therein?

Distance learning technologies are becoming increasingly popular in higher education. Recently in Lithuania it became almost like an obligatory tool in this sphere. For example, in Vytautas Magnus University each university course must have its version in the *Moodle* system. Despite being attractive and especially liked by students, this new trend in teaching methodology is not easily or automatically adaptable to legal education, once again confirming the uniqueness of the latter.

The problem in adapting this technology and methodology is very much visible in the United States. In this country one credit of higher legal education requires 700 minutes of contact hours, which means exactly direct face-to-face contact. American Bar Association, which accredits higher legal studies in the United States, is reluctant to recognize learning in a distant mode (essentially in whatever form) as contact hours. This in itself shows that Americans recognize the impossibility to develop some specific required skills in lawyers without students physically participating in a real-time work in classrooms. These are skills related to practical litigation and adjudication. Everything here is conceived very much like in medical studies – you cannot learn how to operate a patient without really and physically practising it.

The question is that today technologies essentially allow creating conditions of distance learning or studying that are almost equal to physical participation in a real-time work in classrooms. The matter is only the possession of technology and the necessary infrastructure. Regarding this matter, a wide debate is taking place in Lithuania. Usually it is recognized that just going through the *Moodle* version of one or another course is not enough. Legal academia has to start working on how to integrate distance learning methodology into the process of higher legal education, having in mind its special needs, *i.e.* which forms of the new methodology can be considered to be secondary or subsidiary modes of teaching and which forms are appropriate to substitute physical participation in a real-time work in classrooms without damaging the development of necessary skills of the future lawyers.

6 Problem-Based Learning and Feedback to Students: Examples from Scandinavian Legal Education

Ole Hammerslev

In Scandinavia, several law departments and institutions have transformed their pedagogical teaching methods concerning their legal degrees at bachelor and master levels. Traditionally, legal education has been seen as independent self-studies supplemented with lectures and examination requirements.[1]

One of the paradigms that have driven the process is problem-based learning. On the one hand, acknowledging that the legal degrees are mass educations in which not only students coming from families with academic backgrounds study, but that students have diversified backgrounds and different learning methods, and, on the other, that the benefit of lectures is limited, law faculties and departments have transformed their way of teaching from lecturing to problem-based learning with different forms of assessments. In this chapter two Scandinavian models of problem-based learning will be outlined before discussing a form of self-assessment via e-learning.

6.1 Towards Problem-Based Learning at Uppsala University, Sweden

At Uppsala University the legal education was reformed in 1992. The reasons behind changing the education were threefold, and all were based on a survey of law students in Uppsala: (1) students felt as strangers to their fellow students and to their teachers, (2) the students used too many years to finish their education, and (3) the dropout rate was too high. The structure of the degree was thus changed, the degree was more internationalized by offering more international courses, and theoretical and non-dogmatic courses were upgraded. However, the most important factor was the way the actual pedagogical principles were changed as a fundament of the entire degree.[2] The teaching

1 H. Hydén & E. Anderberg, 'Rätten i förvandling', *in* M. Bertilsson (Ed.), *Rätten i förvandling. Jurister mellan stat och marknad*, Nerenius & Santérus Förlag, Stockholm, 1995, pp. 217-251; A. Strandbakken, 'Introduksjon', *in* L.S. Wilhelmsen & A. Strandbakken (Eds.), *Juristutdanningens faglige og pedagogiske utfordringer*, Gyldendal Akademisk, Oslo, 2010, pp. 11-21.

2 H. Eklund, 'En problemorienterad juristutbilding', *in* T. Andersson & B. Lindell (Eds.), *Festskrift till Per Henrik Lindblom*, Iustus Förlag, Uppsala, 2004, pp. 119-128.

was partly transformed to problem-based learning processes based on the students' own activities – such as solving cases and presenting cases – individually and in groups. One impact was that most of the teaching was transformed from lectures to workshops in which the teacher was only a facilitator of the discussions between students. The students should prepare the case before the lessons. In the class a group should present the case and other groups should comment on the presentation. The teacher orchestrated the debates and showed the general lines of the specific legal theoretical background of the problems, which were discussed.

6.2 Problem-Based Learning at University of Bergen, Norway

At the University of Bergen in Norway, the legal education changed in 2003 with the new requirements brought by the Bologna process. The Faculty of Law was challenged by too many students who did not pass the exams, many were taking too many years to finish the legal education, and too many of them dropped out. Besides changing the structure of the legal degree to follow the Bologna model, the focus was to transform the actual way of teaching from lectures, seminars and tutoring to problem-based learning inspired by, among others, Barrows and Tamblyn.[3] With changes implemented, the focus was placed on the students' own learning by changing the role of the teacher from being a lecturer to being a facilitator of the students' own learning processes.[4] One of the most striking changes and innovative teaching methods which were introduced at the legal education at University of Bergen was that the students were divided into groups in which they should discuss different issues in relation to the given problem. To facilitate the discussions, students in later semesters were employed by the university. They facilitated the debates so individual students could be able to finish their own assignment and, moreover, comment on the assignment from the other members of the group. As a further step, the tutoring senior student would give her or his comments to the group. A senior student employed as tutor by the university would follow the same group during the entire study year; this solution would permit the later-semester student, acting as a tutor, to gain knowledge about the students' learning needs. Therefore, tutoring students may fine-tune their teaching approach to the needs of the tutored students.

In problem-based learning the new students will have courses in study techniques with specific focus on problem-based learning, how to take responsibility for own learning, collaboration, reading and writing techniques, etc.

3 H.S. Barrows & R.M. Tamblyn, *Problem-Based Learning. An Approach to Medical Education* Springer, New York, 1980.

4 L.S. Wilhelmsen, 'Masterstudiet i rettsvitenskap ved Universitetet i Bergen', *in* L.S. Wilhelmsen & A. Strandbakken (Eds.), *Juristutdanningens faglige og pedagogiske utfordringer*, Gyldendal Akademisk, Oslo, 2010, pp. 131-150.

Since the introduction of the new study reform, the students' learning profit has increased just as the percentage of students who have completed the degree has increased even though they do it faster than before. Moreover, the students' study satisfaction has increased.

The Bergen model became an inspiration for the later study reforms at the Faculty of Law, University of Copenhagen, and at the Department of Law, University of Southern Denmark.

6.3 Online Self-Assessment and Feedback at the University of Southern Denmark

At the Department of Law, University of Southern Denmark, studies in legal education were established in 2004. It was soon realized that the backgrounds of the students were quite diversified. Many students represented the first generation in their families that had the opportunity to access university studies. As it has been observed, this aspect had some importance in relation to their ways of acting, their self-discipline, their categorizations of social phenomena and their learning approaches.[5] To teach the students to learn and profit at best from their studies, a number of initiatives were taken, *e.g.* courses in study techniques and courses for instructors in pedagogical methods. In particular, the electronic self-assessments should be mentioned. The purpose of these is to give a feed-back to students so that, during the semester, they can test their level and see whether they have understood the specific topics.[6] The assumption behind the self-assessments was that they could target the students' efforts and show the students the purpose of different parts of the subject they were studying. This should not only create a deeper learning but also make the students more engaged and thus give them a greater desire to learn.[7]

The assessments were created in the e-learning platform (BlackBoard) of the university, and they were focusing on the purposes of the courses, namely, on their aim, focus and

5 M. Börjesson & D. Broady, 'The Social Profile of Swedish Law Students: National Divisions and Transnational Strategies', 29 *Retfærd Nordic Legal Journal*, 2006 (3/114), pp. 80-107; P. Bourdieu, *Distinction: A Social Critique of the Judgement of Taste*, Routledge, London, 1984; P. Bourdieu, *The State Nobility. Elite Schools in the Field of Power*, Policy Press, Cambridge, 1996; P. Bourdieu & J.-C. Passeron, *Reproduktion – bidrag til en teori om undervisningssystemet*, Hans Reitzels Forlag, Copenhagen, 2006; D. Broady, 'Förord till den svenska översättningen', in P. Bourdieu & J.-C. Passeron (Eds.), *Reproduktionen*, Arkiv förlag, Lund, 2008, pp. 7-30.

6 O. Hammerslev & L. Hansen, 'Prøver og selvevalueringer: En del af Juridisk Instituts pædagogiske værktøjer', *in* L.S. Wilhelmsen & A. Strandbakken (Eds.), *Juristutdanningens faglige og pedagogiske utfordringer*, Gyldendal Akademisk, Oslo, 2010, pp. 99-121.

7 S. Brown, *Motivating Students*, London, Kogan Page, 1998; S.A. Brown, P. Race, & B.D. Smith, *500 tips on Assessment*, Kogan Page, London, 1996; S.A. Brown, C. Earlam, & P. Race, *500 tips for Teachers* (2nd ed.), Kogan Page, London, 1998; S.A. Brown, P. Race, & J. Bull, *Computer-Assisted Assessment in Higher Education*, Kogan Page, London, 1999.

taxonomical levels.[8] At the beginning of the courses the focus of the multiple choice assessments is on the lower levels of the taxonomy. As the course develops, the focus of assessments changes to higher levels of the taxonomy. In the end the multiple choice assessments becomes highly advanced based on, *e.g.* which arguments would be sufficient regarding judgements in specific cases. One important aspect of the assessments is the response part. The students will get instant and thorough feedback on their answers, namely, whether the answers are correct or not. This is possible because the assessments are created as advanced multiple choice assessments.

6.4 Problem-Based Learning and the Focus on Students' Own Learning

This short text tried to show that in the Scandinavian countries the universities which acknowledged the newest research within pedagogical sciences started transforming their teaching methods in the legal degrees from lectures to various kinds of problem-based learning where the students' own learning activities are in focus.

8 B.S. Bloom & D.S. Krathwohl, *Taxonomy of Educational Objectives: The Classification of Educational Goals, by a Committee of College and University Examiners. Handbook 1: Cognitive Domain*, Longmans, New York, 1956.

7 On the Model of Legal Education in Poland and Its Problematic Evolution

Andrzej Bałaban

Poland as a truly democratic state adopted in 1989 a model of a five-year law studies based on a unitary cycle, currently regulated by the Higher Education Act of 27 July 2005.[1] At their end the student obtains a professional diploma of 'magister' (Master). Over thirty law faculties have presently the power to provide such kind of studies in Poland. Half of them are public universities, and the other half are private higher education schools. The Polish Accreditation Committee at the Ministry of Science and Higher Education[2] supervises the quality of higher education through regular visits to the higher education institutes. The current model of legal studies is not pursued according to the basic two cycles of education envisaged by the Bologna process model (Bologna Declaration). Other studies carried on through unitary cycles are medicine, dental medicine, pharmacy, veterinary, psychology and more. However, Poland implemented other aspects of the Bologna model, for example, the credit system and the related more elastic approach to the programmes, acknowledgement of foreign studies, support of mobility schemes, etc. The existing law school model has been accepted as a basis to file an application to be admitted to exercise the legal profession, starting from a training run by professional corporations of lawyers, solicitors, notaries and bailiffs, as well as to file an application to be admitted, under a competitive examination, to the training as a judge. It is worth observing that the model based upon a unitary cycle master studies in law has traditionally been rooted in the Polish legal culture. This characteristic, in the prevailing Polish conception, relates to the need to guarantee a safe legal circulation, the public confidence of given professions and the requirements of justice.

In the last months of 2012, with the tacit approval of the Ministry, a few universities started to provide simplified legal studies accessible to people with a bachelor's degree in any other discipline. They were at first organized by the Faculty of Law at the University of Gdansk as part-time studies. This generated a lively discussion in the press, in which I also took part, expressing my opinion three times on the front pages of the national newspaper *Rzeczpospolita*, in a tone of protest against the idea and the form of providing

1 The denomination in Polish is: pl. ustawa o szkolnictwie wyższym z dnia 27 lipca 2005 roku.

2 The denomination in Polish is: pl. Polska Komisja Akredytacyjna przy Ministrze Nauki i Szkolnictwa Wyższego.

such studies. In my opinion they are mostly illegal because the provisions of the Act and implementing regulations, which provide the unitary cycle of legal studies, have not been changed. The introduction of these studies relies on the provisions of the Act, which allows faculties having the power to grant the highest scientific grade in Poland, the one of 'habilitated doctor', to autonomously develop a programme of study. This, however, can take place only within the frame of a uniform master studies. Particularly harmful is the gradual introduction of two-level studies as part-time studies. Such studies, which in Poland take place mostly through weekend cycles of lesson, are indeed characterized by a smaller quantity of teaching hours than ordinary full-time cycles. Therefore, it is obvious that such studies are provided in this form only with the highly unethical intention to search for a profit. Indeed, full-time studies are free of charge at state universities, following a constitutional principle, while part-time studies may be provided with a charge.

Breaking the rules of law grows together with a growing interest of other universities to provide this kind of business. Indeed, universities in Poland are generally suffering from a reduction in the registration of new students, mostly due to the demographic decline. The silence of state authorities, especially of the Ministry, can provide for a rapid development of this 'plague'. So far, only the National Council of the Judiciary[3] – the constitutional guardian of the independence of courts and judges – expressed a protest against the new phenomenon. Also in meetings of the Conference of the Deans of the Faculties of Law this problem has been taken up, without any clear findings yet.

Here we see a tension between different positions: (1) the judges' self-government, which aims at protecting the judicial profession, which is made sure by the competence gained through the studies; (2) the state legal faculties, which, on the one hand, desire to make sure that the learning process is provided at a sufficiently high level, but, on the other, need to increase their revenues; (3) the private law faculties, which may increase their turnover through 'innovative' studies; (4) the law professors, who look at the problem from the perspective of not only the quality but also the opportunity. In my articles in the press, I stressed the connection between the possible inflation of such simplified studies and their consequences in the training for the exercise of legal profession. However, we also assist in another legislative phenomenon. Indeed, the Polish parliament undertakes the final steps of the legislative works on the deregulation of about 300 regulated professions involving formal qualification, among which we have in the foreground the legal profession. Following the initiative of some parliamentarians and other politically ignorant subjects, a political group, with strong support from the government, quickly pushed

3 The denomination in Polish is: pl. Krajowa Rada Sądownictwa.

through the legislative process reforms, the aim of which is to liquidate the professional self-government corporations under the pretext of creating jobs for young people. The method of such true destruction is the removal of the existing professional requirements and shortening the procedures for obtaining the authorization to exercise a profession. The Minister of Justice,[4] who pilots this project, even propagated his conception, according to which 2-3 millions of new jobs may be offered in this way. As a matter of fact this tendency may lead only to the collapse of the now existing companies and law firms, as it is already taking place. And right at the beginning, they will start dismissing junior staff. Deregulated professional markets, rather than supporting, hinder in reality the establishment of new businesses and law firms that are not able to pursue those gains which permit to achieve a necessary, even minimum income in the deregulated market. The proposal of deregulation (destruction of self-governments and of the regulated professions), as a typical populist project, distracts from the real reasons for unemployment. It underlines the professional corporations as the common 'enemy', and thus managed to gain the support of the parties of all political orientations, which are even crowding to be near to the deregulation success. There is therefore no hope of stopping the legislative work. The only hope is associated with the possibility of appeal against this second-rate statutes to the Constitutional Court,[5] because they infringe a number of constitutional values, such as the right to give rise to professional communities and self-governments, as well as their autonomy, the right to freedom of economic activity, the right to ownership of the companies (in which deregulation statutes interfere), with the principal protection of acquired rights, the abuse of statutory remedies against economic freedom, of exercise of a profession and others.

It is worth reconsidering the reaction to such populist claims of the legal communities in the universities. The events that took place through the creation of these shortened legal studies trigger discussion in the academic legal communities. However, as it takes place during debates, it shows a group of supporters of these illegal activities, who, as I suppose, are intending to join the financial success of these simplified 'commercial' studies. Such a debate is surely needed; however, it must happen before any reform comes into place. It is in this framework that it may be worth looking at the experience of those European countries that have badly adopted the elements of the Bologna process in legal studies, leading to a deterioration of the quality of the studies. There is no place for reporting the effects of these reforms in different countries as such, but they are not always encouraging. Of course, it is one thing to share the legal studies in two levels, but another thing to admit to the second level of legal studies somebody who took his first cycle of studies in a radically different subject, such as technology. Looking for some comparisons, it is easy to see that, for example, after the first level of studies if one obtains a degree as a

4 The denomination in Polish is: pl. Minister Sprawiedliwości.
5 The denomination in Polish is: pl. Trybunał Konstytucyjny.

paramedic, it is possible to train such a person to become a physician, but would we like to undergo a medical treatment dispensed by an engineer who later became a medical doctor after two years of study and who acquired his 'general' knowledge in the previous studies? The lawyer, by the way, is also a doctor but in a field no less important as justice or the protection of property! Looking at the history of centuries of legal studies and at their present role, which is not so different as before, we should remind supporters of hasty reforms about the saying 'quieta non movere', as if specially created for the assessment of such events.

8 Learning by Debating: About the Project of a New Scientific Journal at the Faculty of Law and Administration of Szczecin University

Marek Andrzejewski

Personalistic philosophy, close to my perspectives, is at present in retreat. Nowadays its important categories, such as meeting of people and face-to-face dialogue, appear less and less attractive. This is evidence of the crisis of the talk, the dialogue and the debate. There is no room here to describe this process, especially since it has multiple complex causes and contexts, which are both global and regional, depend on the nature of local communities, or are generated in certain social or professional groups. It seemed that the Polish pluralistic society, after breaking the chains of communist restrictions, would greatly benefit from the democratic culture of dialogue. Unfortunately, this process took place, but to a degree that is barely satisfactory. Taking advantage of the freedom of speech by those who do not have anything to say, or those who lie or show aggression through word, is rather a problem than a source of satisfaction. A multitude of parallel monologues does not make a debate.

The culture of debate declines in the universities also, to the great detriment of science and education. Academics and scholars less and less frequently meet at seminars, because many of them work a lot, yet mostly on their own. Students have no masters, as many professors do not even aspire such a role, having no time to spare for their students.

In recent years many new scientific journals have been founded, also in the field of law. They are all similar to each other in the sense that you may search in vain for controversies, disputes, etc. even though you cannot deny that the authors have technical knowledge and efficiency in their field. Even when we deal with reviews of PhD dissertations and post-PhD habilitation dissertations, it is sometimes difficult to determine what assessment feed their authors and what is their judgement as to the level of the reviewed studies. The inability to take a position, and perhaps excessive politeness, which is wrongly called kindness, makes the assessments hide behind a wall of words. Additionally, not rare is a phenomenon of writing a 'favourable' review, because of which authors of works of low scientific level receive degrees and titles that they do not deserve. It is also worth mentioning that quite often scholars decline to accept the function of a reviewer once they realize that their review would be negative.

For a few years now the activity of the Ministry of Higher Education has also contributed to a significant degradation of Polish academic life. It is possible to give many examples in support of this claim, which clearly show the reduction of the standards of scientific research. For example, in Poland there are quite a high number of Polish candidates for the highest scientific title, the habilitation, who receive this title in the schools of higher education in those countries where the requirements are not higher than those that we demand in Poland for a doctorate. This regrettable behaviour does not meet any reaction from the Ministry of Science, while the academic community, in turn, is divided with respect to this procedure into a minority, which questions this objectionable behaviour, and a majority, which does not condemn their colleagues for adopting such dubious practices to get a scientific title. This perhaps can be explained by the fact that the universities, although through such a way of conducting said affairs they lower the standards of education, receive from the Ministry a reward in the form of an authorization to provide studies of higher education and sometimes also to grant doctoral diplomas, etc.

In my opinion the Polish scholarly life does not benefit from the adoption and imposition of the system of higher education and the development of science modelled after the so-called Bologna system. Such an approach is widely criticized by the Polish scientific community. Nevertheless, the Ministry has consistently been following 'the only correct line' of development. Legal education has also suffered the negative consequences of such an approach. Indeed, lately in Poland some higher education schools started to provide graduate MA legal studies to BA graduates from any other field. These universities have taken such a decision to provide such education to earn money in the times of economic crisis and demographic decline, although they know that they will be paying for this the price of providing a lower level of education. This method of educating lawyers reminds about the practice adopted in Poland after World War II, when the authorities organized an accelerated legal education to fill in, in a short time, the courts and prosecutor's offices with badly educated, but ideologically obedient communists. After sixty years, the idea comes back, yet this time it does not benefit ideological communists, but ignorant persons devoid of any ideas. Criticism of this approach has not even been heard yet.

At the national annual conference of the society of civil law academics, which was held in Toruń in June 2011, the idea of creating a new civil code was debated. Two keynote papers were presented, one by the late, then 87-year-old, Prof. Zbigniew Radwański and one by Prof. Biruta Lewaszkiewicz Petrykowska, a woman not much younger than the former.

The theses of their papers stood in stark contrast. Yet both spoke clearly, to the point, without malice, without eristic tricks, with respect for each other and the audience, but also with zest. They did not show the slightest doubt that the topic was very important for them and that, to support their theses, put at stake all their great scholarly achievements, knowledge and prestige. Perhaps, in spirit they both were the youngest participants of the conference. I think that that conference was a sign of a certain epoch that was coming to an end. Even if I forget the content of their papers, I certainly will not forget that I participated in a scholarly debate, which so seldom takes place today.

The memory of the Toruń debate allows me to hold back the critical tone of my argument and proceed to formulate some positive thoughts, opposing the present detrimental trends. At this point, also because of the length limitations of this text, I am not able to sketch any comprehensive recovery programme. I may only consider some specific topics, in the hope that this kind of discourse may in time trigger a movement that may lead to improvement of the present situation. In the context of the present crisis of a debate, and therefore also of science and education, with the aim to contribute to their improvement, I would like to offer here, in my capacity as an editor and a researcher, a few reflections about a project – creating a new legal journal in my Faculty.

So far, at the Faculty of Law and Administration of Szczecin University we had a scientific journal that functioned for a dozen of years, titled *Scientific Papers of the University of Szczecin. Legal Yearbooks* [*Zeszyty Naukowe Uniwersytetu Szczecińskiego – Roczniki Prawnicze*]. It was edited and published by the publishing house of Szczecin University. However, in all these years of operation, the journal did not give the expected satisfaction to the editors, the authors, or to the Faculty. It was published in a limited number of issues, because of the decision of the university's delegated authority. It permitted only the publication of a small number of articles. A limited press, and lately only thirty copies, may not be compensated by the fact that the texts were available on the Internet. Bureaucratic release cycle caused growing problems: the publishing cycle, starting from the submission of an article in the publishing house to its printing, took even one and a half years. Thus, instead of satisfaction, it generated frustration in the authors and embarrassment in the editors.

In such circumstances, the idea was born to take the risk of developing a journal without the University publishing house and change the edition formula. The title *Acta Iuris Stetinensis* was preserved.

At the beginning of 2013, the Dean of the Faculty of Law and Administration of the Szczecin University signed an agreement with the presidents of the following institutions of the city of Szczecin: the Court of Appeal, the Regional Administrative Court and the Appellate Prosecutor's Office. The object of this agreement was to jointly issue a scientific journal. The protocol highlighted the need of continuous personal commitment and efforts of all of signatories and their successors in order to publish successive issues of the journal. The parties committed to share the financial liabilities and organizational burden of the project. They manifested the intention that the new magazine should permit the exchange of ideas between researchers and practitioners, and especially those who work in Szczecin and the region. It meant to be an attempt to build a dialogue and cooperation in the research and education, including the debate on the crisis that I mentioned at the beginning of this chapter. In the new formula, the magazine aims to become a forum where theoretical reflection and practice should meet. Besides, it should be aimed at integrating the community of the lawyers of the city and the region.

Just like any scientific journal, the main objective of this one will be the theoretical reflection. I will not develop this thread here, because it is obvious. I would add only that the text of the practitioners, namely, judges, attorneys, counsellors, and prosecutors must also conform to the standards required for the articles published in scientific journals (*e.g.* double-blind review issued by a professor). The Dean of the Faculty promised, whenever necessary, scholarly advice to lawyers and practitioners when preparing their text. The other partners of the agreement pledged to encourage judges and prosecutors to publish in the journal. It was decided to devote a section of each issue, even as wide as a half of it, for the presentation of judgements delivered by Szczecin courts and other courts operating in the region, including commentaries drawn by scholars and experts from Szczecin and other places. In the long term, it would be worth trying to create a web-based database of judgements, to publish monographic issues of the journal joining selected decisions and commentaries and to organize conferences on subjects that are meaningful both for theorists and practitioners. We aim also to present the opinion of scholars in the form of articles and interviews on the different issues raised by practitioners. We are convinced that this initiative can contribute to a better application of the law, and it can also improve the process of lawmaking.

The regional character of the journal would also be manifested by the presentation of the events characterizing the life of the legal institutions, which are not so much known to the general public. Among them there would be information about habilitation debates and lectures, doctoral defense, important court cases, etc.

The ambition of the creators of the new formula of the journal is therefore not only to underscore its regional character. We will make an effort to have it read not only by scholars, judges, prosecutors, lawyers, counsellors but also by the students, research students, and candidates for the legal professions. Our ambition is that the journal may serve the development of education and lifelong learning and research, enhancing at the same time the sense of community of lawyers.

The idea presented may not look extremely original, but since there is not a journal of this kind in Poland, we feel it is important to concentrate on the idea.

We are preparing this new formula of journal strongly believing that we are right when examining the need for a broader legal education and the need for a growing exchange of ideas – especially between practitioners and theorists of law. But we also know that our idea goes against the current directives issued by the Ministry of Science. Ministerial policy – implemented through financial pressures – encourages the production of legal texts for the achievement of points awarded according to the rules, which may be reasonable for the sciences. The regional magazines and the debates we aim to develop are not among the categories valued by our Ministry.

According to the decision-makers, the greater the score of a journal, the fewer the articles written by authors from its own environment. In contrast, the value of the journal rises when we have a majority of the authors from other legal environments, especially when some of them are writers from abroad. In Poland, bonuses are also awarded for foreign reviews and texts in English, which should be surprising if we take into account that we are talking about a Polish journal addressed to Polish readers. Polish law topics may be significantly alien to people who do not know Polish reality.

However, when doing what we consider to be right, we need to take into account the reality, which is also composed by the Minister. We need therefore to act pragmatically also because the Faculty is subject to the assessments formulated by the Ministry. This assessment in turn affects the financial support to the Faculty.

However, we intend to criticize ministerial rigors concerning publishing magazines, including absurd criteria for their evaluation, but we will also try to get the highest possible ministerial rank. We will therefore create a scientific board of the magazine to include independent and well-known academics from Poland and abroad. We will apply for affiliation in the international database. All articles will be subjected to a double-blind review, and no fewer than the required 24 articles will be published annually, which will be also available on the websites of both the Faculty of Law and Administration of the Szczecin University, as well as on the websites of our partners, etc. In short, we will try to fulfil all other requirements that the Ministry will surprise us with. As I am writing these words, the publishers and the editors of scientific journals are waiting for new criteria for evaluating journals to be prepared by the Ministry, which in recent years have changed more often than the release cycle of yearbooks.

We would like to devote our energy and strength to this initiative, to help create the opportunity to be able to experience, also in the future, events that would have a form of scholarly debates such as the one mentioned above, which took place during the congress of civil law specialists in Toruń.

Part III
Court Administration and Legal Profession

9 Court Administration as a Practice and as an Academic Discipline

Philip Langbroek

9.1 Courts as Professional Organizations

The classic professions are medicine, law and theology. The professionals are medical doctors, lawyers and priests and reverends. During the past 30 years in the United States and in Europe we have seen a development where professional organizations like the police, schools, hospitals, universities and courts have transformed from institutions with leadership based on professional skills to professional organizations with an increasingly professional management.

Especially where courts traditionally have been understood as one or more judges hearing and deciding a case, the development of courts as professional organizations has challenged traditional constitutionalism and traditional public administration - traditional constitutionalism, because it has not dealt with court administration in a meaningful sense, apart from the demand that judges be independent from other state powers and impartial towards the parties at a case filed at the court. Traditional public administration was challenged because traditionally it left court administration to lawyers. From an academic perspective, this has left an open space. Traditional constitutionalists have claimed that judicial independence requires an absolute autonomy for courts as organizations in relation to other state powers. While the specialists in public administration gathered evidence for the perverse effects of new public management in public organizations,[1] policymakers have applied new public management also in court administration, for example, in France (Charte Marianne), in England and Wales and in the Netherlands (output financing of the courts). The constitutional debate about court administration is about the way courts are being governed and the participation of other state powers in this activity. Therefore, where more administration is involved in the management of courts and judges, a focus of attention is the internal relations between administration and judiciary in general, and management and judges within the court organization. This is confirmed by jurisprudence of the ECHR, which also explicitly states that internal influencing of judges is contrary to demands of judicial independence and impartiality.[2] This should,

1 John Seddon, *Systems Thinking in the Public Sector*, Triarchy Press, 2008.
2 ECHR *Agrokompleks v. Ukraine* (Application no. 23465/03), 8 March 2012.

however, not be seen as an imperative from the ECHR that judges cannot be subjected to management. They should be left uninfluenced in their dealings with concrete cases. Even so, modern organization developments in court organizations do strain the relations between judicial autonomy and court organization.

9.2 SEPARATION OF POWERS AND ACCOUNTABILITY

Separation of powers has never meant an absolute independence of the courts. Courts are part of the state organization and are financed with public money. Legal arrangements for budgeting and accounting, therefore, are unavoidable. In a traditional European construction the budget for the courts is part of the budget of the Ministry of Justice. The way in which money for the courts is spent and the expenses which take place are controlled according to the budget discipline and accounting rules by the Ministry of Finance. The Minister of Justice has political responsibility for the court administration. This means not only defending the budget for the courts in parliament but also buffering political criticism on judgements in the political debate. The alternative is that the judiciary administers itself and proposes a budget bill to parliament and is itself accountable for its spendings, such as the federal judiciary in the United States. It has been amazing to see the development of a Ministry of Justice in England, together with a ministerial political responsibility for the administration of justice and a separate position for the Lord Chief Justice as the head of the judiciary, into almost a European continental model. In the states of the German federation a debate is also going on about the position of the judiciary. In its current state the superior appeal courts are responsible for the governance of the courts within their district, but they are accountable for their administrative functioning to a Ministry of Justice. In the Netherlands the Ministry of Justice and the administrative council for the judiciary have to cooperate to make the court governance work. This is a cooperation not only in the budgeting and accounting process but also regarding legislative measures for the functioning of the courts. Although in France the Ministry of Justice centralizes court administration, in several 'Départements' local courts administer new ways of organization and cooperation within the judiciary. In southern countries, such as Italy and Portugal, Councils for the Judiciary provide for human resources policies for the judiciary. This enhances, on the one hand, judicial independence, but on the other, also makes the work of the Ministry of Justice as court administrators much more complex because of inflexibilities in judicial positions.

In all jurisdictions a major issue is the relation between judges and the law. In continental Europe this regards the relation between the judiciary and the legal rules. Whereas in the French revolutionary ideology, judges should just implement legal rules, the relation between judges and the law seems less a relation of subjection in the Anglo-Saxon legal systems.[3] There, judges are not so much seen as civil servants but rather as office holders with a separate mandate to uphold the law. It seems that this approach has consequences for what concerns court administration. In Europe the political grip on the judiciary seems much larger than in the United States. But even there, at the level of the Members States of the federation, the relation between the judiciary and politics is characterized by some tension. To see how those tensions work out, it is sufficient to refer to the extensive public questioning sessions in the American congress for the appointment of the judges in the Supreme Court, as well of the federal chief justices. Still, in US politics, there is a clear and evident respect for the (federal) judiciary and its independence.

9.3 Court Administration and Management

The question, what is necessary to make courts function as they should? is, to some extent, autonomous from the general structures conceived for the administration of courts and judges: courts should indeed be not only independent and impartial but also efficient and timely, with a clear view of societal needs. That is not so simple, because courts do many different things with relevance for quite some different social fields. Problem-solving courts can have a major neighbourhood influence; small claims proceedings are important for ordinary people and for providers of small services in large numbers such as phone companies. Trade cases and the way they are handled may have an impact on a wider economic scale. Criminal cases have a wide public appeal, and in public discussions the difference between suspect and convict runs the risks of being neglected, but it is essential for the functioning of justice with a two-sided sword – to establish the right facts and to decide on guilt or dismissal of prosecution or acquittal of the suspect. Here some major problems for court organizations become visible.

9.3.1 Impartiality and Independence Ethics

Everything a court does is being affected by the demands for judicial independence and impartiality. The courts are expected to have their internal logistics in order. Logistic aspects are important for both efficiency and timeliness perspectives. Timeliness is an ethical issue, because letting parties wait more than about nine months for an outcome of their case is socially unacceptable. There may be exceptions for the most complicated cases, but letting citizens wait longer is not the kind of service they are entitled to. There are always

3 J.H. Merriman, 'The French Deviation', *The American Journal of Comparative Law* 1996, pp. 115-125.

many reasons to delay a case, but usually those reasons have everything to do with the court organization or with professional traditions, like in several Italian courts, where the first case management decision is to postpone the hearing of the case.[4]

This is a matter of not only shifting files at the right time to the right place but also monitoring the progress of a file and taking measures to speed up preparations for hearing and decision-making. Often this process is speeded up by making use of ICTs in the shape of a case flow management system, where paper files have been replaced by e-files and where cases can be filed at the court online. However, such an approach presents a few moral issues related to the allocation of cases to the judges. In most countries this has not been arranged for by law as, for example, it has been arranged legally in Italy and Germany.

Legal regulation of the allocation of cases means, for example, that negotiations with advocates or prosecutors about setting the date for hearing are out of the question. Advocates know the court; they know, for example, when a strict judge will be on a holiday and may try to get a postponement and another judge assigned to the case. Also court staff needs to be instructed on this and should be loyal to the court, not to the advocates. Professional ethics therefore should be ingrained in everybody working in the courts. That is not self-evident, and support for professional ethics requires an open organizational culture, where colleagues can discuss ethical issues instead of being threatened by sanctions if they make a mistake.

9.3.2 Case Allocation

In first instance courts, different types of cases are dealt with in large numbers. This requires court staff and judges to apply working routines while staying alert for special circumstances. This is not so easy. Similar cases should be decided similarly. Also at the same time the complicated cases that may make it up to the court of cassation or to the Constitutional Court should be dealt with. Considering the rapid developments in law, in society and in technology, this also demands that courts take care that judges and court staff know enough of the new developments in order not to be overwhelmed by super-specialized advocates. On a wider scale, it is inevitable that a national court administration takes notice of this need for knowledge management and organizes courses for judges and court staff. Because of the enhanced transparency of the courts as organizations and the work of the judges, this may also be taken on a national scale. Traditionally the uniform application of

4 *E.g.* L. Verzelloni, 'Behind the Judges' Desk: An Ethnographic Study on the Italian Courts of Justice', *International Journal for Court Administration*, Vol. 4, No. 2, 2012, pp. 3-4.

the law is assured by appeal and cassation in continental legal systems. However, the number of cases that is being appealed is at present about 10% of the total, whereas the number of cases that reaches the stage of cassation is much smaller than that proportion. Judges and court administrators therefore face the challenge of verifying that similar cases are dealt with similarly on a national scale as well. Of course, national guidelines or standards (*e.g.* for sentencing in criminal cases) may be of help. But also here the independence and impartiality issue plays a role: who is to set those standards? Is it enough to rely on the professional knowledge of the judges? Should they be supported somehow?

9.3.3 *Public Relations*

Media attention is one of the most difficult challenges for the courts. Journalists may want to film in the courtroom, but this often does not fit the parties or the court. There are symbolic qualities to what happens in the court room that may be diminished or broken by intrusive media coverage. A small remark of a judge or a party can be blown into gigantic proportions by repeated media broadcasting. On the other hand, court hearings are public in principle. So the courts must find a delicate balance between media exposure and protecting the interests of the parties of cases. Furthermore, judgements are given in writing, often in complex legal language. Journalists often lack time for a proper reading of those judgements and they may need support from the court to understand the outcome of the case.

Public criticism on court decisions is of all times. In a constitutional state, politicians may propose to change the law if they do not agree with the outcome of a judgement. This often happens because of loopholes in taxation laws. There is nothing wrong with that. On the other hand, the general public may also take part in a debate. If a popular politician is prosecuted, or if a mistake has been made by a court, it may be of great importance that the general public is informed about what the courts do. Public relations has become an important task in court administration, and it is questionable if each separate court can organize its own public relations. It depends on the court size, but there may also be a national or regional public relations policy.

9.3.4 *And Much More: Quality Management*

Other aspects of court work concern the security in the court buildings or the design of court buildings to strictly separate judicial office quarters from public spaces, personnel policy, internal budgeting policies, management of relations with the bar and with the public prosecutions office and organization development.

A tool for organization development is quality management. This means that everything a court does is organized in concentric circles: planning, acting, checking, reacting *ad infinitum*. Customers of the courts and personnel are to be actively involved in this. Part of quality management and public accountability of the courts is the handling of complaints. This aspect is of importance, because complaints must be distinguished from disagreement with a court decision.[5] Sometimes judges do not treat parties or advocates according to standards. Advocates often are very reluctant to file a complaint because they feel maltreated. However, for a good court performance, it is essential that judges also receive feedback on how they have managed a case during hearing.

9.3.5 *Court Organization as Part of Local Society, and Innovation in Legal Education and Training*

Completing this short survey, we shall not neglect the relation between court and local society. As we have been looking at the court administration as a key element to connect the court activity with the society, we shall also take into account that organization of the court is also a part of the local society. Courts fulfil quite an essential social function in this respect. For that reason it is essential that the court is made visible to the local public, and, if necessary, is able to adapt to pressing local needs. Problem-solving courts can be seen in their local environment as a part of a national experiment. It is also possible to engage such courts in activities of flexible cooperation with, *e.g.* the prosecutions office, the police and, as a matter of example, a youth protection agency. Also here judicial independence and impartiality should be kept in mind; however, they should be used as conditions to be fulfilled instead as obstacles for flexible cooperation.

However, a key element in an open approach of the courts as organizations is the interaction between courts and the different corporations and institutions within their jurisdictions. Among such corporations and institutions are, for example, the bar associations, other free associations of lawyers, youth care agencies and law schools. Law schools have a special importance for the court, as they provide research and training and are able to analyze problems, which may be of practical importance to the courts. Furthermore, through the appropriate organization of court practices and of joint practical courses, law schools and courts may share the burden of learning how the court functions and how for example constitutional principles but also rules of procedure are operated and implemented in court practice. Legal studies are based in principle on

5 H.P. Pauliat, 'The Treatment of Citizens' Complaints in the Justice Field: Is an Ombudsman Necessary?', *International Journal for Court Administration*, Vol. 2, 2008, pp. 33-42.

curricula, which are unitary in the sense that, notwithstanding specialization, all legal studies are provided by institutions, such as law schools, which have similar aims and provide similar methods of learning for all the candidates of the legal profession. So there is no rivalry, protection of specific interests, and there is no effort to show consensus in public. We already mentioned such interactions in the former parts of this contribution. This means that courts ought to include the issues related to their interaction with the outside world in their organization policy. Also, law schools should be open for involving parts of civil society in seminars or conferences they organize or even involve them in their courses. In this way, a tendency to debate all dimensions of the life of the lawyer, which may also involve the active parts of the civil society, including magistracy and lawyers' associations, may more easily develop, with respect to the identity of the interlocutors, but enhancing the public and transparent dimension of the discourse on the essence of constitutionalism in the measure in which it has to be safeguarded by the judicial process.

9.4 Conclusions

Summing up, court administration has become a separate field of attention for academics and policymakers. Societal demands and pressures on the courts have become so intense that the old institutions had to be transformed into complex organizations, which need help from professional managers to deal with the burden of increasing tasks. This involves cooperation between judges and managers/administrators. Their collaboration leads to the development of policies on a national scale. Information management, public relations, development of an ethical code, working relations with the bar, enhancement of the predictability of judgements in similar cases, continuous vocational training, specialization policies and human resources management, research and development: there is practically no end to all the activities serving to enhance a better functioning of courts and judges.

9.4.1 More Research Is Necessary

For academics and researchers this evokes numerous questions. For example, are judges able to withstand pressures for more efficiency? Do austerity measures go at the detriment of the content quality of judicial work? Are policies to enhance predictability of judicial decisions acceptable from a judicial independence perspective? How far does organization development in court administration allow the judiciary to fulfil their counterbalancing function in the constitutional state? Does organization development in court administration give politicians in the government more power over the judiciary? Is there a risk that the judiciary is transformed into an instrument of a democratic and Jacobin majority rule?

Those and other questions can only be answered by research where lawyers, sociologists, political scientists and economists cooperate.

To answer those and similar questions and to exchange information about what way of court administration works best, several networks and platforms have been developed.

9.4.2 A Map of Scholarship

To enhance scholarship in court administration as well as to support the relations with the civil society, it is also necessary to enhance systematic exchanges between judges, court administrators and scholars. There is, for example, the International Association for Court Administration,[6] which organizes such platforms in its conferences and in its journal, the *International Journal for Court Administration*[7] and the *Justice Systems Journal of the National Center for State Courts.*[8] In Europe, there is the EGPA study group on Justice and Court Administration,[9] which organizes exchanges between practitioners and scholars once a year during the annual EGPA conference. The study group's area of interest is very diverse and can deal with issues such as judicial governance, court and case management, statistics, judicial budget and planning, records and space management, information and communication technology, performance assessment, delay reduction programmes, quality of justice, ethics, corruption, fundamental rights, mediation, therapeutic jurisprudence and so on. The study group is connected with The Research Institute on Judicial Systems (IRSIG-CNR)[10] of the Research Council of Italy in Bologna, Italy; The Observatory for Justice, of the University of Coimbra, Portugal[11]; The Research Centre for Judicial Studies of the University of Bologna, Italy[12]; and The Institute of Law and Technology, Universitat Autònoma de Barcelona in Spain.[13] Another related project, managed by Dr. Daniela Piana from the University of Bologna with more than 40 partners, is the Menu for Justice project, seeking to make an inventory of best practices in training for lawyers and judges.[14]

Also taking part in the study group is the Synergia project on Justice Management, based in Switzerland, managed by Prof. Andreas Lienhard and Daniel Kettiger. This project seeks

6 <www.iaca.ws>. All websites mentioned in this contribution were accessed on 2 January 2013.
7 <www.iaca.ws>.
8 <www.ncsc.org/Publications/Justice-System-Journal.aspx>.
9 <www.iias-iisa.org/egpa/e/study_groups/justice/Pages/default.aspx>.
10 <www.irsig.cnr.it/>.
11 <http://opj.ces.uc.pt/>.
12 <http://www.dsps.unibo.it/it>.
13 <http://idt.uab.es/>.
14 <https://www.academic-projects.eu/menuforjustice/default.aspx>. The Menu for Justice project is financed by the Erasmus programme of the European Commission.

to enhance the knowledge in Switzerland on court and justice management. Switzerland is a country of diversity on a relatively small scale. For that reason the outcomes of the Synergia project in the next few years will also be interesting. The questions being asked within the project are being approached in an interdisciplinary manner. I quote from the website <www.justizforschung.ch>: "In order to gain insight into the judicial system from the outside, the interaction of legal, sociological, macroeconomic, psychological, historical, and politology aspects are being considered. Furthermore, research related to the judiciary's mode of operation, its organization and internal processes, and the interaction among the persons working within the system can be conducted only within an interdisciplinary framework. The structure of the research project – corresponding to several recognized management models – is divided into a study of the internal organization of the judiciary, on the one hand, and its surroundings, on the other. The study related to the internal organization deals with the elements of resources, processes, organization (structure), and culture". The project is based on a multidisciplinary cooperation between the Komptenzzentrum for public management in Bern,[15] with the Universities of Zurich,[16] Lucerne,[17] St. Gallen,[18] Idheap[19] and the Montaigne Centre of Utrecht School of Law in the Netherlands.[20]

Last, but certainly not the least, we refer to the European Commission for the Efficiency of Justice of the Council of Europe,[21] which also organizes studies and exchanges of experience in court administration amongst judges and court administrators of 47 Council of Europe Member States.

15 Prof. Andreas Lienhard and dr. Daniel Kettiger, <www.kpm.unibe.ch/content/research/research_projects/fundamental_principles_of_good_judicial_management/index_eng.html>.

16 Prof. Giovanni Biaggini, <www.research-projects.uzh.ch/a817.htm>.

17 Prof. Michele Luminati, <www.unilu.ch/eng/luminati_michelefachbereich_9580.html>.

18 Prof. Kuno Schedler, <www.unisg.ch/Wissen/Faculty?current=8&person=B9F626A4-9606-411F-AE9F-952357C9501D&name=Kuno_Schedler>.

19 Prof. Yves Emery, <www.idheap.ch/idheap.nsf/vwBaseDocuments/U4Act01?OpenDocument&lng=en>.

20 Prof. Philip Langbroek, <www.uu.nl/montaigne>.

21 <www.coe.int/cepej>.

10 The Role of Disciplines Concerning Management and Organization of Judicial Systems in Legal Education and Judicial Training

Luigi Lepore

10.1 Introduction

This contribution aims to stimulate an open debate on the composition of curriculum of European students of law faculties, both within the academic community and between people that work in, and around, judicial systems. In particular the chapter tries to analyze the actual and the potential role of some 'non-legal' subjects, such as *Public Management*, *Public Administration*, and other specific disciplines concerning topics of management and organization of judicial systems and their organizations (*e.g. Court Management*, *Judicial Administration*).

An open debate around some questions regarding the potential role of managerial disciplines mentioned above seems to be needed, because it could bring some advancement in the sensitive issue of innovation in legal education and training. Undoubtedly the discussion conducted in the chapter reflects the opinion of the author, which, probably, is in contrast with the common culture surrounding the judiciary. In this way, the chapter and particularly the consequent debate could contribute to address a fundamental problem of the present times: How to put legal studies and legal training in the conditions to innovate?

10.2 Traditional and Innovative Non-Legal Disciplines in the Curriculum of European Students of Law Faculties

Research activities conducted during the carrying out of the project Menu for Justice – Toward a European Curriculum Studiorum on Judicial Studies[1] seem to show that the

1 For further information, please refer to <https://www.academic-projects.eu/menuforjustice/Pages/Project.aspx>.

complexity and the evolution of modern court administration need a set of skills and expertise that traditionally are not part of traditional judicial training almost in all European countries.

Data collected through the questionnaires administered in some law faculties of the countries involved in the project mentioned above show that 'legal' subjects are the core of the undergraduate law degree in Europe, despite the presence of 'non-legal' subjects becoming important in many countries. In fact, more and more often some 'non-legal' subjects are provided as mandatory in the curriculum and/or as optional. In particular, 62% of the countries analyzed had some 'non-legal' disciplines as mandatory for the students, while in 81% of the countries students have the opportunity to choose some 'non-legal' studies as optional. Sometimes 'non-legal' disciplines are also present in the interdisciplinary courses. In 48% of the countries analyzed there are mandatory courses that combine another discipline with law. In the 67% of the sample this kind of courses are present as optional.[2]

Precisely, it is possible to identify seventeen most common 'non-legal' disciplines (see Tables 10.1 and 10.2). Some of them could be defined 'traditional non-legal disciplines'; the rest are 'innovative non-legal disciplines'. Apart from the nature (mandatory or optional) of the subjects, it is possible to collocate disciplines that are present in the majority of law degree courses of the countries surveyed in the first group. It is the case of *Economics*, *Political Science*, *History*, *Foreign Language*, *Research Method*, *Medicine*, and *Philosophy and Ethics*. Instead, disciplines present only in some countries could be located in the second group: *Accounting*, *Public Management*, *Public Administration*, *Management and Organizations of Judicial System* and *Sociology*.

Table 10.2 shows in a more analytic way the different 'non-legal' disciplines that constitute the curriculum in European law faculties. *Public Management* and *Public Administration*,

Table 10.1 Traditional and Innovative 'non-legal' discipline in legal studies

Traditional	Innovative
Economics	Accounting
Political science	Public management
History	Public administration
Foreign language	Management and organizations of judicial system
Philosophy and ethics	Sociology
Medicine	
Research method	

2 For further information, please refer to TF 1 report 'Initial legal studies in Europe', *Menu for Justice* report.

Table 10.2 'Non-Legal' Disciplines Taught in European Law Faculties

Country	<u>PS</u>	<u>EC</u>	*Soc*	<u>His</u>	<u>FL</u>	*Acc*	<u>P&E</u>	*PA*	*PM*	Psy	S&M	*M&O JS*	Ant	<u>Med</u>	<u>RM</u>	Comm	EP
Austria	O	M		O	M	O	O			O			O	O	M	M	O
Belgium	O	M	M	O	M		M	O	O	M	O				O		
Denmark			M/O		O		M										
England and Wales	O	O		O	O		O				O		O	O	O	O	O
France	M	M		O	M		O								M		
Germany		O			M	O				O				O	O		
Hungary	M	M		M			M				M			O		O	
Italy	M	M	O	M	M	M/O	O	M/O	O	O	O	O	O	M/O	O	O	
Iceland				O	O					O			O	O			O
Ireland	O	O			O					O							
Latvia	M/O				M/O									O	M		
Lithuania	M	M		M	M		M			M			O	O	O	O	O
Malta	O	O		O	M		M			O	O		M	O	O	O	M
Romania							M					O					
Slovenia		M		M/O	M									O	O		M/O
Spain	O	M															
The Netherlands	O	M/O		O	O		O			O	O		M	M	M	M	M
Turkey	M/O	M/O		M/O	M/O		M/O			O	M/O		M	M	M/O	M	M
Total M&O (no. of times discipline is present)	**<u>13</u>**	**<u>14</u>**	***3***	**<u>12</u>**	**<u>15</u>**	***3***	**<u>12</u>**	***2***	***2***	10	7	***2***	8	**<u>12</u>**	**<u>12</u>**	8	8

Type of courses	
M	Mandatory
O	Optional
M/O	Mandatory and optional, depending on the university
Frequency	
<u>Bold U</u>	Disciplines more frequent
Bold IT	Disciplines less frequent

Disciplines	
PS	Political sciences
EC	Economics
Soc	Sociology
His	History
FL	Foreign language
Acc	Accounting
P&E	Philosophy and ethics
PA	Public Administration
PM	Public Management
Psy	Psychology
S&M	Statistics and Mathematics
M&O JS	Management and organizations of judicial system
Ant	Anthropology
Med	Medicine
RM	Research Method
Comm	Communication
EP	Environmental Policy

for example, are present as optional in Belgian and Italian universities; *Public Administration* is also present as a mandatory course in some Italian universities. *Management and Organizations of Judicial System* is taught in Romanian law faculties as an optional course. In an Italian university students have the opportunity to study topics related to *Management and Organizations of Judicial System* as mandatory courses of *Economia Aziendale* (lit. *Business Administration, but see infra*).[3] *Accounting* is present as an optional discipline in Austria and Germany, while in Italy it is optional at some universities and mandatory in others. *Sociology* is taught as a mandatory discipline in Belgium and Denmark; it is present as an optional in Denmark and Italy.

As is clear from Table 10.1, disciplines concerning public management, public administration, and/or other topics regarding the management and organization of judicial systems are not considered very important. There is, in fact, a common orientation in the countries surveyed about some 'non-legal' disciplines (traditional non-legal disciplines), but there is no similar common orientation regarding other subjects (innovative non-legal disciplines).

10.3 A New Era in Legal Education and Judicial Training?

Considering this 'state of the art' of education for law students, and also taking into account that sometimes the non-exciting performances of judicial systems (*e.g.* in terms of timely resolution of cases) are due to a lack of organization and management skills of personnel involved in the managerial functions and in the administrative activities of courts,[4] it seems to be clear that a more careful debate should begin about the role of disciplines

3 *See* 'The case of Parthenope University' in TF 1-report 'Initial legal studies in Europe', *Menu for Justice* report.

4 D. Oglesby & G. Gallas, 'Court Administration – A New Profession: A Role for Universities', *America Business Law Journal* 1971; R.W. Tobin, *An Overview of Court Administration in the United States*, NCSC, Williamsburg, VA, 1997; C. Baar, 'The Development and Reform of Court Organization and Administration', 19 *Public Administration and Development* 1999; M. Fabri, *Processi di modernizzazione organizzativa, gestionale e tecnologica della giustizia, l'esperienza degli Stati Uniti d'America, in Quaderni*, CESORG, 1991; M. Fabri, *Amministrare la giustizia. Governance, organizzazione, sistemi informativi*, Lo scarabeo, Bologna, 2006; S. Zan, *Tecnologia, organizzazione e giustizia*, Il Mulino, Bologna, 2004; B.J. Ostrom, T.M. Clarke, R.Y. Schauffler, C. Ostrom & R.A. Hanson, *A Unifying Framework for Court Performance Measurement*, Final Report, NCSC, Williamsburg, VA, 2008; L. Lepore, 'Efficienza, efficacia ed equità nell'amministrazione della Giustizia', *Azienda Pubblica*, 3/09, Maggioli, Rimini, 2009; L. Lepore, R. Agrifoglio & C. Metallo, 'Measuring the Performance of Italian Courts: the Role of IS Success', *in* M. De Marco, A. D'atri, S. Cabiddu & A.M. Braccini (Eds.), *Management of the Interconnected World*, Springer, Berlin, 2009; L. Lepore, F. Alvino & L. Borrello, '*ICT and Judicial Administration: A Model for the Classification of E-Justice Innovations, in* M. De Marco, Dov Te'eni, V. Albano & S. Za (Eds.), *Information Systems: Crossroads for Organization, Management, Accounting and Engineering*, Springer, Berlin, 2012; L. Lepore, C. Metallo & R. Agrifoglio, 'Evaluating Court performance: Findings from Two Italian Courts', *International Journal For Court Administration* 2012.

concerning public management, public administration, and other topics regarding the management and organization of courts and judicial systems.

In the United States, at the beginning of the 1900s, a growing popular dissatisfaction with the administration of justice and the consequent increasing demand for efficiency of operations within court system put in evidence the need for the beginning of a "new era in judicial administration".[5] Both in academia and among judicial operators it was emphasized that judicial system suffered from a lack of up-to-date procedure and standards for administration and management of courts, putting in evidence the need of administrators and court staff trained in management. Courts were in general managed by a presiding judge and a clerk, who did not have formal training in management. So specialized court management education and training became imperative. As a consequence, universities and law schools began to organize courses and master's to teach court management and judicial administration.[6]

In Europe there is not a long tradition of scientific study and training in court management. However, the fact that it is increasingly becoming an important topic is shown by the activities carried out by the Cepej (European Commission for the Efficiency of Justice) to improve the quality of European judicial systems, and also by the increasing number of studies conducted in Europe on the topic of court management.[7]

What happened in the United States could be developed in Europe today to improve the quality of justice if, or where, it is true that courts are overwhelmed with civil and penal cases, if, or where, it is true that the bad performances of judicial systems in terms of quality of justice are due to organization and management problems. In these situations,

5 Oglesby & Gallas, 1971, p. 2.

6 Ibid.

7 For further information, please refer to P.M. Langbroek, 'Reinventing the Least Dangerous Branch of Government: Judicial Independence and the Accountability for the Administration of Justice, Courts and Judges in The Netherlands', *in* M. Fabri & P.M. Langbroek (Eds.), *The Challenge of Change for Judicial Systems. Developing a Public Administration Perspective*, IOS Press, Amsterdam, 2000; Zan 2004; D.C. Steelman & M. Fabri, 'Can an Italian Court Use the American Approach to Delay Reduction', *The Justice System Journal*, Vol. 29, No. 1, 2008; Lepore *et al.* 2009; L. Lepore, 'Court Management e controllo manageriale dei Tribunali', *in* F. Alvino & L. Lepore (Eds.), *Efficienza, Efficacia ed Economicità del Sistema Giudiziario italiano: la prospettiva economico-aziendale*, ESI, Napoli, 2010; L. Lepore, *Il sistema giudiziario italiano nella prospettiva economico-aziendale: governance e controllo*, Albano, Napoli, 2011; L. Lepore, R. Agrifoglio, C. Metallo & F. Alvino, 'Un modello per la valutazione delle performance dei tribunali: un'analisi empirica', *in Azienda Pubblica* 3/10, Maggioli, Rimini, 2010; L. Lepore, F. Alvino, C. Metallo & R. Agrifoglio, 'Learning and Knowledge Sharing in Virtual Communities of Practice: A Case Study', *in* A. D'atri, M. Ferrara, J.F. George & P. Spagnoletti (Eds.), *Information Technology and Innovation Trends in Organizations*, Springer, Berlin, 2011; Lienhard, D. Kettiger & D. Winkler, 'Status of Court Management in Switzerland', *Internationl Journa for Court Administration*, 2012 .

probably new sound management principles, logics and instruments should be introduced, and court staff, court managers and maybe presiding judges should be trained to use these innovations. In the modern court administration, in fact, increasingly often courts deal with issues that are not strictly legal and addressable through knowledge of the law. These organizational and managerial issues require expertise in such areas as case flow management, budgeting, accounting system, information management, human resource management, performance indicators, etc.

Therefore, in other words, we shall urgently consider whether or not it is necessary to give more emphasis on these topics. Is it useful or necessary to promote managerial professional skills of court workforce, lawyers and judges? Is it necessary during the undergraduate level of education or in the graduate level, PhD programmes, vocational training? Bearing in mind the modernization and homogenization processes involving the European Union on several fronts, is it useful to introduce a common group of 'innovative non-legal teachings' in the curriculum, like what happens today for legal disciplines? This is, of course, without deleting the peculiarities of the teachings provided in each of the different countries, individually considered, which are still necessary because they reflect the specificities of each cultural context. Considering that selection processes of judicial leadership for courts are often based on seniority, is it useful or necessary that, in the future, selection methods for judicial leadership explicitly consider organizational and managerial skills and competences?

However, we repeat, the aim of this chapter is not to give answers to the questions mentioned above but to stimulate a debate, starting from the opinions of the author, in particular on what concerns the potential role of managerial subjects mentioned, innovation in legal education and training.

Finding answers for these questions is certainly not an easy task, but a more thoughtful conversation should be conducted, not only in the academic world but also among judicial actors. Today more than ever, it seems important to assess the key gaps in legal and judicial education in all European countries at all stages of education, from undergraduate to graduate and PhD programmes, to vocational training of lawyers and judges.

One of the main troubles is that innovation in legal education and training is a sensitive issue. It involves indeed a lot of questions, *i.e.* on the different judicial cultures of every country, on differences in the legal systems and on relationship between independence of judicial system and the need of accountability for courts and, more in general, for judicial systems.[8]

Despite difficulties and problems mentioned above, however, if the introduction of managerial and organizational disciplines into the legal education and judicial training can contribute in some way to improve the performances of European courts in terms of efficiency, effectiveness, equity and quality of justice, thus avoiding problems of justice delayed, then legal education of European students of law faculties and training of courts administrative personnel, judges and lawyers should be reviewed as soon as possible.

10.4 The Case of the Faculty of Law of Parthenope University

The Faculty of Law of Parthenope University in Naples is offering a wide and comprehensive programme of higher education that includes an innovative discipline for law students: *Economia Aziendale*. It concerns topics regarding public management, business administration in general and other issues of management and organization of judicial systems and their organizations. The Faculty of Law of Parthenope University was founded in 1999. Now it includes a large number of scientists who work in different areas not only related to the traditional disciplines taught in law faculty. Among them we find Public Management, Business Administration, Public Administration, Organization, Human Resource Management, etc.
For some years, some of these scholars focused their interests on some topics regarding judicial administration, court management and its instruments (accounting systems, information systems, etc.) applicable to Italian courts. Doing so, they studied the judicial systems in the perspective of public management. Their main research themes include performance measurement of courts and judicial systems; efficiency, effectiveness and equity of courts and judicial system; economic dimension of the court activities; accountability and accounting systems; organization; e-justice; information systems and organizational change in judicial system; information systems performance evaluation; etc.

The development of innovative research on these issues stimulated innovation in education as well. In fact, as mentioned above, today the law degree courses offered by Parthenope University include a discipline named *Economia Aziendale* that can be described as a mix of public management and business administration, which aims to provide students

8 The issue of independence and accountability has been addressed in the academic debate, and the need for accountability principles for courts compatible with the fundamental principle of independence seems to arise (Ostrom *et al.* 2008; Langbroek 2000; F. Contini & R. Mohr, 'Reconciling Independence and Accountability in Judicial Systems', *Utrecht Law Review*, Vol. 3, No. 2, 2007; Lepore 2009). It is fundamental for a court and for a judge to be independent of any kind of possible influence, such as social, political and economic pressure. But it also is fundamental for a court, as a public institution, to be efficient, effective and accountable in the use of public resources.

with lessons on management and organizational aspects related to the judicial system as a whole and to its individual institutions (*e.g.* courts).

Within the course of *Economia Aziendale* (9 credits – 72 hours) students gain insight into issues such as accountability and independence of the judiciary; efficiency, effectiveness and equity of judicial system, courts and people (judges and administrative staff); performance measurement; organization; accounting systems; economic dimension of court activities (analysis of costs and revenues). The course also addressed issues relating to the judicial reform process initiated by the legislator, exploring the themes of autonomy, responsibility and control of/in the judicial system.

The topics mentioned above are addressed in both a theoretical and practical perspective. For example, issues of efficiency and effectiveness, as well as those of performance measurement, are addressed by not only providing students with theoretical knowledge but also analyzing the instruments for measuring these dimensions (performance measurement system, accounting system). In this sense, the judicial system as a whole, as well as individual courts, are regarded as non-profit organizations whose performance must be analyzed for the sake of their improvement.

Part IV
Towards a Space of Experimentation for Legal Training

11 The Order of European Integration, the Coexistence and the Interaction of Constitutional Orders in Multilevel Framework: Teaching the Passion for Legal Protection in a Complex World

Pasquale Policastro and Teresa Freixes

The reasons to provide higher education over the centuries have been related to different motivations, which may be synthesized into two: (1) the development and the strength of the political system[1] and (2) social promotion.[2] Although these elements are closely

1 Ancient Greek schools of philosophy permitted to master knowledge, both general and applicative. In particular, they led to the creation of the cultural framework, allowing to consolidate the power of the city states. In this sense speculative knowledge and practical know-how went together with a specific frame of mind. From R. Parry, *Episteme and Techne, The Stanford Encyclopedia of Philosophy*: "even Aristotle refers to technê or craft as itself also epistêmê or knowledge because it is a practice grounded in an 'account' – something involving theoretical understanding. Plato – whose theory of forms seems an arch example of pure theoretical knowledge – nevertheless is fascinated by the idea of a kind of technê that is informed by knowledge of forms. In the Republic this knowledge is the indispensable basis for the philosophers' craft of ruling in the city"; *see* <http://plato.stanford.edu/entries/episteme-techne/>.

2 The development of the University of Naples by Friedrich II Hohenstaufen, King of Sicily and Head of the Roman Empire, a 'state university' giving a training, ending with a profession title (granted from the sovereign), as well as creating a regulated community, where the mobility of the studies was not possible as in the other universities. From the web pages of the University of Naples 'Federico II', we have a summary of the conception of the sovereign of Sicily to found "a university whose teachers he could select and whose regulations he could deliberate on, in contrast with the totally free and spontaneous process, initiated by both teachers and students, which had presided to the formation of the first European universities in the previous decades" <www.unina.it/ateneo/cenni/cenniStoriciEnglish.jsp>. This approach, which aimed to stress clearly that the role of the legal education had to be conceived in function of the national state, was the element of another 'legal revolution', namely, the development of an approach where the monarch was the legislator, supported by a professional administration. *See* J. Berman, *Law and Revolution. The Formation of the Western Legal Tradition*, Cambridge, MA., 1983; It. Edn: Diritto e rivoluzione. Le origine della tradizione giuridica occidentale, Bologna, 1998, p. 386-387, Italian edition The consolidation of the power had a very strong relation with the promotion of better conditions of life. The monarch had the duty to maintain public order and administrate justice. His power to enact statutes was clearly affirmed. He was assisted by a professional administration. In practice, the power of the monarch was limited by the different communities. Here the influences, also international, of the merchants, could not be neglected (*see* Berman, 1998, pp. 390-92). The question here of the accountable improvement of the 'prosperity' of a community became a part of the political agenda.

intertwined, and therefore most of the functions of higher education may be studied starting from the interdependence between them, we may find at least one element that develops from the connection of these two motivations, namely, the promotion of a clear understanding between persons: we will call this motivation (3) developing comparable understanding of the phenomena.[3]

This dimension is extremely important, especially for the present Europe. Indeed, university in Europe, as it emerged from Middle Age, gained its identity when it was able to develop a form of reasoning, namely, recursive reasoning, which was stemming from the experience of Indian Buddhist colleges *vihara* and Islamic colleges, called *madrasa*. So besides the characteristic of European universities to consolidate the political transformations,[4] or to promote a tolerant attitude in the government, and therefore rights,[5] we see that in Europe this model was consistent with a fragmentation of law and of legal profession. Therefore, notwithstanding the common Roman roots of law in Europe, which individually were celebrated by each university in different occasions, the phenomenon of development of professional corporations, which was also rising from Middle Age, overwhelmed, with its centrifugal tendency, the centripetal tendency to the unification of knowledge stemming from the identification of reasoning. In the legal field the consolidation of the national states became associated with the formation of the lawyer, and of the legal professions, which was strictly national. Notwithstanding the common Roman roots, fundamental unity of phenomena such as the development of constitutionalism in Europe and the impact of French Revolution on the constitutional political orders of the different Member States, phenomena as important as codification of civil law remained constrained within the metalanguage of the general categories. Comparative law was used only for knowledge purposes or when the transnational character of specific events was calling for it. It remained outside the experience of each lawyer. The tendency was the centring of the legal culture on the national experience. The contacts with external legal experience were only functional to the widest possible extension, or the widest possible protection of the national experience. At the internal level, the unification of the jurisprudence of the courts, a significant problem, and later on the hierarchization of the rules with constitution on the top, produced different dogmatic approaches to legal reasoning.

3 C. Beckwith, *Warriors of the Cloisters*, Princeton, 2012.

4 Berman, *1998*. A quotation of Berman, what we would call the 'syllabus' of Odofredus (pp. 151-152, Italian edition), shows the practical implication of the disputation approach. Odofredus wrote, "First I will make a summary of each title [of the Digest] [. . .] Second, I will give examples of each statute [included in the title] as clear as possible [. . .] Third, I will review the text, with the aim to correct it. Forth, I will shortly repeat the content of the examples [. . .] Fifth, I will solve contradictions by means of general principles" (free translation in English by PP). This syllabus shows the 'scientific' approach to law, by means of reasoning.

5 M. Stolleis, *Staat und Staatsräson in der früihen Neizeit: Studien zur Geschichte des öffentliches Rechts*, Frankfurt, 1990 (Italian edition: *Stato e ragion di stato nella prima età moderna*, Bologna, 1998).

Legal professions centred on the national experience. The differentiation of the *ius dicere*, even though substantively not big, was enough to differently enact law. They were enough also to differently understand law, starting from the universities. To prepare for the legal profession became isomorphic to law.

This process, on the European ground, created an artificial and sometimes paradoxical situation. Considered in general scientific and philosophical terms, this process may be tested according to the hypothesis of the relativity of categories.[6] This hypothesis states that the linguistic patterns determine what the person perceives in the world and what the person thinks about it. However, this possibility has been verified in the cases of human cultures where the basic elements of the knowledge process, like the Kantian forms of the intuition (time and space), and the categories of the intellect, such as substance and causality, appear quite different. This is not the case in European cultures, and in particular in European legal cultures. However, each student of comparative law knows that culture, history, society, language, the interaction with different cultures and with specific phenomena and problems produce a different approach to law, to legislation and to the solution of legal cases. These elements are, furthermore, key factors to determine the characteristics of legal dogmatics and legal reasoning. This in turn influences the didactics and the handbooks.[7] Furthermore, legal and political theories have proposed a paradigm of legal knowledge and institutionalism (S. Romano, Hauriou, Weinberger and, more recently, La Torre), which relates legal experience and finally even subjective validity to the cultural perception of the legal order. Institutional theory poses the accent on the coexistence of legal orders, which together give rise to complex legal cultures. The political decision to create a common market first and then the complex process of creating an ever closer union among the peoples of Europe produced the need to take into account ways and methods to produce a legal order out of the legal orders, which were interacting. The jurisprudence of the European Court of Justice had an enormous contribution in this regard. Fifty years after the seminal decision in Van Gend and Loos and some months after the Nobel Prize for Peace for European Union, we acknowledge the process of European integration related to the development of common spaces of individual freedom, of economic freedom and of rule of law. In this creation, the functional and gradualistic founding elements stay alive through the need to develop integration by means of progressive achievements. Such perspective is important because it does not lead to a final consolidation of the process of European integration in principle, but opens it to periodic

6 L. von Bertalannfy, *General Systems Theory*, 1955, 1969, Chapter 10, referring to Whorf and others.

7 P. Policastro, 'Zasady podstawowe w zagranicznych podręcznikach prawa konstytucyjnego – perspektywa europejska' [The Fundamental Principles in the Foreign Handbooks of Constitutional Law – A European Perspective], *in* A. Bałaban & P. Mijal (Eds.), *Zasady Naczelne Konstytucji RP* [*The Fundamental Principles of the Constitution of the Republic of Poland*], Szczecin, 2011.

verifications that take place through the development of treaties and legislation. This permits the European Union legal order to evolve and approach issues of key importance. Among them, we have the protection granted to European nationals and to third-country nationals and the protection granted to formal and to substantive freedom. In this perspective, we see that the jurisprudence of the Court of Justice of the European Union can protect the freedom of movement of services, when related to the exercise of legal practice, only to a very limited extent. In this field, the limitation of the range of European competence and the limited efforts of the Member States to develop a full awareness to give to the exercise of profession a full-fledged European range result in the fact that legal profession does not yet have a full European dimension. This finally jeopardizes the competitiveness of this profession in the global markets and the development of European law firms which are able to profit from the importance and the significance of European legal heritage. Furthermore, it limits the development of the space of European integration as a space characterized by a substantive respect of common standards concerning the rule of law. The latter aspect is becoming increasingly important for further European integration.

The progress of the process of European integration through the development of a legal space characterized by a common standard of protection of the rule of law and a substantive protection of freedoms needs the integration of modelling efforts and legislative efforts, as well as adequately formed lawyers. Indeed, the development of the protection of a common standard shall take into account that in the process of European integration we deal with the coexistence of different national legal orders, which develops through the mediation of different factors. Among such factors, we have the interaction with the European Union legal order and the order of the Council of Europe. However, since each legal order has its own constitutional phenomenology, the mediation, which permits their coexistence, has also its own constitutional transformative (we denote this as dynamic influence[8]) influence over national legal orders. For this reason the lawyer, who has to deal with such a normative order, needs to be trained in a specific way, which takes into account such different interactions.

The coexistence of different legal orders, of different legal cultures, influences indeed all the aspects of law, starting from the constitutional principles. Such principles are especially important where they are embodied in models permitting the understanding of how legal orders mutually relate. By constitutional principles we intend the three following

8 P. Policastro, 'Interdipendenze costituzionali e protezione della persona', *Scritti in Onore di Luigi Arcidiacono*, Vol. VI, 2011, p. 2635 *et seq.*; P. Policastro, 'Constitutionalism vs. Economic Analysis: On the Use of Founding Theories and Complementary Theories in Constiitutional Interpretation', *Interdisciplinary Research in Jurisprudence and Constitutionalism*, S. Kirste, A. van Aaken, M. Anderheiden & P. Policastro (Eds.), *Archiv für Rechts- und Sozialphilosophie*, 1/2012.

classes of legal principles and values: (1) the aims of the societies; (2) the principles that distribute the influences on (a) the society, (b) politics and (c) production and distribution of income and wealth; and (3) the modal principles, which determine the modality through which the binding character of law manifests. This modelling of constitution is developed to deal with a comparative approach built (1) on a time perspective, affected by constitutionalism and the conformation through time of its three evolutionary paradigms; (2) on a plural perspective related to the coexistence of different models simultaneously; and (3) on a vertical perspective, related to the coexistence of different levels of legal experience, such as the one determined by (a) habits (themselves of different levels and nature); (b) legislation enacted by representative bodies to govern a polity; (c) constitutional principles, which rule aims at distributive and modal principles of a polity; and (d) rules aiming to permit the coexistence of the variety of different complex valid orders structured on the hierarchy between constitution and statutes.[9] However, the development of a conception of the constitutional principles designed to even a conception which is especially developed for comparative issues needs to be put into practice.

The training of the lawyers, as developed in the perspective of one university, will be finally influenced only by the legal mediation of the national state where the legal education takes place and, eventually, by its interaction with the European legal order. The quantity of European supranational and international aspects, which are taught, does not in principle improve the situation, since it is only through taking a conscious distance from a specific national experience, and through the effort of developing a multi-prospective multilevel approach, that we may develop a training of the lawyers that may be able to approach the European experience in its complexity – a lawyer who may enrich the different national perspectives with the law of European integration. For this reason, in this endeavour the importance of modelling the process of European integration is paramount.

The different conferences and research projects, including 'Jean Monnet' activities, the Regensburg conferences on European constitutional law and, to a more limited extent, conferences of the Centre français de droit comparé, permitted to join the paradigm of research just presented with other paradigms of research. In this way were produced the conditions to apply these findings to didactics. Apart from the paradigm of research stated

9 P. Policastro, 'Political parties – participation and representation face to globalisation, European Integration and democratic transformations', *in* M. Granat, P. Policastro & K. Sobczak (Eds.), *Partie polityczne we współczesnym konstytucjonalizmie*, Lublin, 2001: in this article my first version of the theory of the 'paradigms of constitutionalism' appeared; P. Policastro, *Prawa podstawowe w demokratycznych transformacjach ustrojowych*, Polski przykład, Lublin, 2002: in this monograph a theory was used to explain the constitutional transformation in Poland; P. Policastro, 'Constitution and Conflict', *Marmara Journal of European Studies*, June 2012 (forthcoming): here, the approach to the 'paradigms' of constitutionalism has been fully adapted to the comparative analysis of the constitutions, also in an enlarged framework of reference.

above, other paradigms of research also joined. One of them was based on the development of integration of the legal orders by means of substantive and transversal principles. This paradigm, developed mainly at the Jean Monnet Chair in European Constitutional Law at the 'Universitat Autonoma de Barcelona', with a significant didactic application, especially at master's and PhD levels, took up the function to coordinate the project of developing a new joint master's in Law and Policies of European Integration. There were also the paradigm of research of the discursive theory of democracy, the substantive approach to democracy, developed at the university of Montpellier and at the College de France, the paradigm of the constitutional dimension of governance, developed at the State University of Milan, the paradigm of the coexistence of different legal orders in European constitutional law, developed at the University of Regensburg and the above-mentioned paradigm of the static and dynamic interdependence of the legal orders, which was developed in Szczecin. We shall note that all these paradigms of research are related to the 'coexistence' of plurality of legal orders of different legal nature. They are all related to the interaction of different types of legal orders, with the aspects of life having constitutional relevance. Therefore they are related to the multilevel problem, and the relation between constitution and constitutionalism. However, such paradigms constitute autonomous and, in some cases, distant approaches from the one (Pernice) who made use of the denomination 'multilevel constitutionalism' for the first time.[10] We acknowledge, however, the importance of such an interesting formulation, which became a shield under which many different considerations and evaluations could develop.

The consortium which gave rise to the European Master in Law and Policies of European Integration: European Constitutional Law and Multilevel Constitutionalism was therefore founded with the aim to develop a coherent didactic approach to European constitutional law studies, as a means to coordinate, without unnecessary reductionism, the legal complexity arising from European legal integration. A constituent decision was to choose the development of the formula of the 'joint diploma'. The reason behind this choice was related to the importance to grant an equal responsibility and an equal importance to all the partners, as well as to all the different knowledge of the legal phenomena. Therefore, while the founding universities had to grant a joint diploma, the consortium opened to a number of associate and cooperating universities from several countries belonging to

10 This paradigm permits one application on the different subjects, directed to search a pertinent interpretation and application of the international and EU law in the internal level (national or regional). *See* T. Freixes, 'Multilevel Constitutionalism Equality and Non Discrimination', *in* S. Kirste, A. van Aaken, M. Anderheiden & P. Policastro (Eds.), *Interdisciplinary Research in Jurisprudence and Constitutionalism*, with M. Sales, 127 *Archiv für Rechts-und Sozialphilosopie* 2012, and 'Multilevel Constitutionalism as General Framework for the Ascertainment of the Legal Regulations in the European Union', *in* J.L. Pérez Francesch (Ed.), *Libertad, seguridad y transformaciones del Estado*, Institut de Ciències Polítiques i Socials, Barcelona, 2010.

European Union and to the Council of Europe, and with a policy that addressed the widest enlargement possible of the perspectives presented. The didactics had to be founded furthermore on a full mobility of the teachers and the students, and on a full bilingualism: the courses and the examinations had to be taken in English and French, the two languages of the Council of Europe. These hypotheses of work from the same founders appeared both innovative and courageous. Anyway, the programme Socrates acknowledged the importance of the project and granted a support for two years to prepare the project of the new studies.
The final agreement was undersigned only by four of the five participants of the project for the Socrates grant. They were the Universitat Autonoma of Barcelona, which coordinated the grant; the State University of Milan; the University of Montpellier I and Szczecin University. The University of Regensburg did not enter into the agreement as a partner giving the joint diploma. The debate, which was developed within this consortium, concerned the foundations of the Bologna process and, to some extent, also the principle of subsidiarity. Indeed, the remark was that the legal studies in Germany were ending with a state examination giving right to exercise the legal profession. The question appeared very problematic since it appeared to be related to the hypothesis of the relativity of categories. Indeed, the argument set forward by German partners on several occasions seemed connected to the issue that, to pass the state examination, one needed to have a deep knowledge of German law. Such knowledge may be acquired in principle only through a dogmatic approach to law, which could be given only through the German language. While we may not deny that a part of the German legal experience occurs through categories of German language and culture, the experience of the making of European legal cultures and the one of their interactions within European integration have a very significant bulk of common elements. To deny it seems to be, in our understanding, to deny the very essence of law.

The limitation of the European legal experience using the national cultures approach as *la pensée unique* or as a 'wall of separation' between self-consistent, self-sufficient and parallel approaches, *qui superiorem non recognoscent*, is denied by many experiences, which have been inspiring the development of the programme of the course of our European master's.

The first semester, which has been taking place in Barcelona, has four modules: (1) the legal foundation of European integration and government of complexity, (2) fundamental rights and gender, (3) liberty and security in social Europe and (4) Spanish and Catalan language and culture. The teaching modules in the second semester, the lessons of which have been taking place in Montpellier for one year and in Milan the next, are as follows: (5) guarantees of the rule of law and democracy, including also citizenship issues; (6) legal culture of European Union, including among other things its '*acquis*', loyal cooperation and subsidiarity; (7) the multilevel principle in the perspective of territorial representation and relations between institutions; (8) French or Italian language and culture. The modules taught in Szczecin University, which has been hosting the third semester every year, are as follows: (9) principles of the integration of the legal orders in Europe, including the relationship between legislation and enlargement process of the European Union, as well as legislative and jurisdictional methods for solving the conflicts between the legal orders; (10) the relations between decision-making and European policies, including the deliberation process of European institutions, and the control over the transposition of directives; (11) economy of European integration and the importance of the technological society in the process of European integration, including some introduction on the use of artificial intelligence methods; (12) Polish language and culture. In the fourth semester the students take their own practice and complete the writing of their dissertation under the supervision of the master's lecturers.

The institutional teaching programme, as we can see, is chosen following a problem-based approach, which takes into account the interrelations between the legal orders, within the process of European integration, taking into account elements that have a fundamental meaning for constitutionalism, such as the relation between the rights and their protection, the relation between representation and participation, the relationship between norms (on paper) and their practical interpretation.[11] Furthermore, they are organized to show to students the development of the standard of protection of the rights and freedoms in Europe, in a way which permits their practical application. The method of teaching by means of problem-solving has been related to an approach based on a gradual practical teaching on writing legal acts, such as writing a recourse to the European Court of Human Rights, a summary of a legal decision of a European court, up to more complex activities, such as commentaries to legal decisions of the Court of Justice of European Union and of the European Court of Human Rights, individual or group in-depth analyses, writing court press communicates, writing legislative acts, especially directives, simulating deliberations in the process of approval of European legislative acts. Furthermore, the lessons have been enriched with scientific debates and seminars, provided also in teleconference. It has also integrated a gender perspective in the entire academic activities, with a transversal consideration of equality and non-discrimination (mainstreaming), thus supporting the overall objectives that the European Commission has proposed in its action "Gender and Science". The purpose has been to enrich the programme with the presentation of the state-of-art scientific research in the main field of study, also in an interdisciplinary perspective, including workshops on new drugs, nanotechnology and society, climate change, Islamic and ethical banking, peace and nuclear weapons ban.

11 See the paradigms of constitutionalism mentioned above.

All this activity has been made possible through the contribution of a wide range of lecturers and a wide range of universities and scientific institutions associated to or cooperating in the project. Indeed, apart from the partners providing a whole didactic semester or hosting the discussion of the dissertations, we had lecturers, and therefore cooperating universities, from Belgium, Finland, France, Germany, Great Britain, Holland, Italy, Poland, Portugal, Spain, Russia, Sweden and Turkey. Apart from that we had also guest lecturers from Iraq, Malaysia, Senegal, Syria and United States of America. We also had workshops trying to present legal practice in different forms, invited representatives of institutions and law firms of NGOs and paying visits to various institutions. This cooperation with the 'real world' created several opportunities for the students, both for their practice in international ambits and for their working possibilities. In addition, students have been effectively integrated into research projects at universities, thereby obtaining a real experience in research activity.

The European Master in Law and Policies of European Integration: European Constitutional Law and Multilevel Constitutionalism, based upon its policy of full mobility of students and of professors, has been trying, through the didactic process, to lead to a close integration of the agendas of the different universities. A significant number of research projects were developed between all the partners in the two years of preparation and in the five years of the functioning of the master, reinforcing, on a network scale, the relationship between legal research, didactic process and professional training.

The recruitment of the students has been, however, easier for those countries that applied the Bologna system, namely, a first-level diploma of three years, followed by a second-level diploma of two years, and a third-level diploma related to three years of studies and research. The training and the teaching of students coming from a political sciences experience and law studies experience together has been a stimulating opportunity to experiment interdisciplinary mehtods and approaches. Indeed, the master's itself can be a good opportunity, according to our experience, to discuss the development of interdisciplinary degrees and the coordination between the specific needs of training for legal profession and complementary interdisciplinary knowledge. Furthermore, the master's experience has been a very good opportunity to consider the importance of integrating students from different countries and of organizing studies on a multilingual and a multicultural base. The master's indeed has been attended by students of Azerbaijan, Belgium, France, Germany, Italy, Poland, Réunion, Spain, Slovakia and Sweden. The didactic mobility in four countries has permitted their training to study in different countries, while the full mobility of the professors has permitted to achieve a didactic process where the issues related to European integration have been presented from different perspectives. Therefore, the students have been able to develop a wide range of interests, which has led them to search and obtain practices in Italy, Poland, United States of America, Saudi Arabia, Mexico, Brazil, Russian Federation, Spain, Belgium, and, therefore, speeding up their access to job market and their career, which for most of the graduates from the master's started under the best auspices.

The didactic and the scientific experience related to the master's has posed a number of perspectives concerning further innovation in legal education. The first one is the importance to go beyond the studies provided only in one university and centred on one methodology or approach, however declaratively international or comparatist. We expect, however, that the transformation of the universities into network-based universities may not be a process starting from above. It would be inconsistent with the historical development of the universities and with the importance acknowledged to civil society for European integration. From this follows the necessity to overcome the mere national system of accreditation of the studies in favour of sharing competences with a European agency (to be created),[12] eventually through a parallel agreement between European Union countries – an agreement which may be open, in its characteristics, also to non-Member States. The Master in Law and Policies of European Integration: European Constitutional Law and Multilevel Constitutionalism, started as a transnational activity, may show the way to new forms of supranationality starting from the bottom and fully consistent with the spirit of the Bologna process.

12 [. . .] with more powers than the present European Network for Quality Assurance in Higher Education <www.enqa.eu/>, which was established in 2000 to promote European cooperation in the field of quality assurance, following the recommendation of the Council of 24 September 1998 on European cooperation in quality assurance in higher education (98/561/EC). The differences between the systems, and sometimes the distortions we observe in the adaptation to Bologna process, in the different countries, as we have been seeing in the chapters of Andrzejewski and Bałaban, at least for what concerns the Polish example, showing that such developments would be highly suitable.

12 Towards a Supranational Dimension of Citizenship Through Knowledge, Skills and Competence: From ECONET to the Great Green Wall*

Pasquale Policastro and Emilio Castorina

The establishment by the universities of transnational study programmes and interdisciplinary curricula by means of networks may lead to the development of a new wave of revolution in the European culture and society based upon knowledge. This process may be most suitable for constitutionalism, since it may naturally spread the values of active citizenship and responsibility for the common good. It may also disseminate the values of the acknowledgement of the same extent of legal protection to individuals, especially in cases where different legal orders interact. This is markedly the case where individuals who are not citizens of European Union get in contact with the European Union legal order. However, this is also the case when legal situations, which are not yet in the domain of a harmonizing competence of European Union, become functional in substantively fulfilling European constitutional competences. An important issue is related to research, innovation and education, which are still mostly the object of national competences. Here the question is that policies developed by polities normally address the benefit of the horizon of interest related to the polity itself. For this reason enacted policies are not necessarily pursuing the common good of all the polities, which are interacting. From this arises the importance of supranational or transnational processes. Their significance relates to their

* The chapter, although in its general features concerning ECONET developments is the fruit of the strict cooperation of the authors in interdisciplinary issues, has been developed by Pasquale Policastro. The authors, as coordinators of the Scientific Board of ECONET, would like express their gratefulness to Mark Entin, for the cooperation extended to the ECONET summer schools. For what concerns the interdisciplinary issues, the reference authorwould like to thank Ornella Corazza for the very important cooperation granted within the ReDNet project, Kesra Nermend for allowing the integration of the students of the European Master in Law and Policies of European Integration: European Constitutional Law and Multilevel Constitutionalism, in the Case-Study Creator, Barbara Wąsikowska, Agata Wawrzyniak and Krzysztof Bogusławski for the readiness to integrate students in the creation of expert systems permitting to join telemedicine to Prevention and Control of Psychoactive Substances. A special thanks to Djibril Diagne for the support and encouragement given to our students and us, regarding the participation in the Great Green Wall, as well as to the young volunteers who participate in the reforestation in Senegal and in other African countries. Their attitude and dedication provided us with the necessary stimulus to conceive an innovative process of education ranging beyond European Union and addressing the common good.

viability and their possibility to involve different groups beyond national and regional borders. Indeed, since supranational competences in the field of education, and in particular in the field of legal education, are still not clear, the development of international and supranational initiatives may be supported by the power of involvement of different initiatives coming from below. This is the reason which justifies the need to develop synergies between the European space of higher education and experimental activities planned by universities and other institutions as transnational networks. For this reason, following the idea to pursue, through research and advanced training, the full potential of the global dimension of European constitutional integration, the first conception of ECONET, Centre of Research and Advanced Training in European Constitutional Law, was developed. According to the Agreement of Association, written in 2006,

> [t]he present process of European integration joins with the growing enlargement of the EU and the diffusion of the general principles of European constitutionalism. Such diffusion gives to the process of the development of the European legal culture a Northern, Eastern, Western and Southern dimension. Such dimensions have to be led to an adequate convergence. These questions are of great interest for the legal science, and highlight some problems for the development of a legal culture on a global scale, inspired to different values, namely: the respect of the human dignity and of the human rights, understood as legally binding principles in the national, international and supranational spheres; the respect of the principles of democracy based upon participation, the dialogue and law as the sole instruments to arrive to the solution of politically relevant questions; the respect of the limitation of the public powers and of their use in order to promote the full development of the human person in a spirit of peace, dialogue and tolerance; the participation of the individual subjects, of the groups and of the communities; the implementation of the principles of human dignity and of the coordinated exercise of the private and public activity; the promotion of the dignity, of the freedom and of equality in every legal relation and in every legal order, in a dynamic process of overcoming the formal and substantive discriminations. Such questions are, each of them, a challenge for the institutions that specifically deal with the teaching, the training and the research.

For this reason, the founding Members undertook to take together efforts to explicitly join research, training and practical contribution to policy- and legislation making.

Concerning the project of the network, we aimed to develop an open network directed to embrace and join different methodologies of research, didactic and practical action, as well as different contributions: the participation in projects of research, the development of summer schools, of joint activities addressed to debate political transformations and new legal developments, as well as integrating networks of students with scholarly activities. The open network approach, since it allowed a different extent of participation, permitted to keep integrating scientific contacts, leading them to the creation of further consortia, as it has been the case with the European Master in Law and Policies of European Integration: European Constitutional Law and Multilevel Constitutionalism, or as it been the case in the relations with the Institute of European Union at MGIMO University of Moscow.[1] Furthermore, the open network approach permitted the development of a number of projects, which the authors and the members of the scientific committee of ECONET considered to be important for the future, but demanded wide interdisciplinary teams. The development of the needed task forces would have required, however, a significant time and energy. The schools ran by ECONET permitted the development of the seminal work, which, in due course, has led to the formation of a structured team being a condition to begin a genuine comparative and, at the same time, interdisciplinary research. This produced with time a significant potential for innovation in legal education. Indeed, all the schools organized by ECONET so far have had a clear comparative foundation attempted to produce innovation in legal education. The first school, concerning the relationship between the idea of political autonomy and freedom of the persons (2007), had indeed in mind to go towards a conception and a practice of protection of the person, which would range beyond the understanding of the person and the possibility of protection characterizing a specific polity and a given legal culture. The second school, Language and Constitution: a Key Issue for European Integration (2008), following previous attempts to highlight the problem, started to consider how to produce methods which may be useful to promote the precise transfer of legally relevant meanings from one legal system to the other. This approach was related to the relationship between the subject that tries to give a meaning to law and law itself. It linked law to the cultural background and to the neural functions of the subject who deals with it. As time passed by, the reconstruction of such legal 'semiosphere' (Lotman)[2] became connected with the context where law applies, with special reference to the contemporary

1 'Amplius in Castorina', P. Policastro (Ed.), *Liberty and Language. The Constitutional Dimension of European Constitutional Integration*, Torino, 2011, pp. 7-12. The quoted book work also involves the proceedings of the first three schools of ECONET.

2 *See* P. Policastro, 'Constitutionalism, Comparison, Complexity: Prolegomena on Liberty and the Use of Language for a Predictive Theory of Law', *in* Policastro 2011, pp. 15-109. The 'sieve' reported in appendix has been designed as a tool for the comparative reconstruction of the legal semiosphere. For what concerns Lotman's works, *see* M. Lotman, 'Three Functions of the Text', *in* M. Lotman, *Universe of the Mind: A Semiotic Theory of Culture*, translated by Ann Shukman, with a foreword by U. Eco, Bloomington and Indianapolis, 1990, pp. 11-19.

technological society. This generated an interdisciplinary cooperation, which has been leading so far to study how *e.g.* telemedicine, scientific approaches to fight against drugs, transfer of technology between universities and companies and the related support to the development of new companies may generate a cooperation between students of law and students in other fields such as economy, medicine and technology already during their university studies. The importance of this methodology is related to the aim to enhance the blend between knowledge, skills and competence (see the European Communication of 2008, for the European Qualifications Framework) at any level of superior knowledge, in a natural and participate way.

The third school of ECONET addressed 'Interdependence and substantive freedom in post-capitalistic world', and involved students of the University of Catania and the Moscow State Institute of International Relations (MGIMO). The first part took place in Catania, in summer 2009, with a strong presence of an international and diversified team of lecturers.[3] The second took place in Moscow in October 2009 and was based upon the participation in the public debates of the summit between European Union and Russia, which were organized at the MGIMO University. In this school the address towards the achievement of knowledge, skill and competence led to the search of methods compatible with the European approach to legal education. In particular, the method of simulating a problem in a complex negotiation, taking into account roles and unknowns, an approach normally applied to train diplomats, has been used and verified. Following the school, other initiatives have been taken, developing further interaction between ECONET and the students. In particular, the attempt to join knowledge, skills and competence led to open ECONET to a wider cooperation with the students. On this subject the project PEACELAB had a significant influence. This project, which was presented in the ECONET summer school of 2009, may be defined as a knowledge-based platform serving to integrate the development of high-level knowledge with its practical implementation, involving skills and competences. According to the original formulation of PEACELAB (which was presented in the summer school of 2009, by P. Policastro), we intend "PEACE as the ground of a transnational rule of law, based upon the protection of the existential manifestations of the life of the human person, participation and responsibility of each actor, political transnational dialogue, and the grounding of the economic development on activities serving to restore the equilibrium between mankind and nature, and to satisfy the fundamental human needs". Therefore, the project itself aimed at the progress of knowledge in law, implementing such knowledge in practice through the development of skills addressed to propose new legislations, in the context of the knowledge-based society. It aimed also at becoming

3 From Russia, Japan, USA, Germany, Sweden, Spain, Italy, Switzerland, Austria, Turkey, Poland.

the ground to enlarge the competences in transnational politics, mainly through the creation of synergies with other projects of research and NGOs.

The structure of PEACELAB permitted to integrate students within its activities. We may present here the example of the members of the 'scientific circles' of students created at Szczecin University, Faculty of Law and Administration, as a way to integrate legal studies with practical activities. In particular, projects were developed that addressed the writing of texts of directives, permitting to develop legislation writing techniques and to operate with different levels of impact assessments. Through these activities the students of the PEACELAB scientific circle could develop activities in an international environment, for example, in cooperation with the students of the European Master in Law and Policies of European Integration: European Constitutional Law and Multilevel Constitutionalism. The writing of directives permitted to develop policy reflections on the basis of the 'Baltex' project[4] and a participation of the students together with their supervisors in the project 'ReDNet' (Recreational Drugs European Network), coordinated by the University of Hertfordshire.[5] ReDNet was aimed at developing an information platform and a system of early warning for novel psychoactive substances.

PEACELAB also participated in an interdisciplinary cooperation with the said university of Hertfordshire, West Pomeranian Technological University (Academic Centre of Computer Science) and Szczecin University (Faculty of Law and Administration, Faculty of Economics and Management). Such a cooperation, developed under the coordination

4 Which permitted a considerable interdisciplinary interaction between students and researchers. Indeed the days 29-1/09/2010 the University of Szczecin organized a scientific workshop dedicated to the climate change issue and its effects on the natural and socio-economic environment of the Baltic area. The session had an interdisciplinary character and was organized through a special cooperation between the Faculties of Law and Administration, Earth Sciences, Sciences of Hearth, Economic and Management Sciences as well as the Western Pomeranian Scientific Society. Scientists from Poland, Lithuania, Estonia, Sweden and Germany discussed together with students from the international master's programme Law and Policies of European Integration: European Constitutional Law and Multilevel Constitutionalism the function of the climate system, and the pressure and chances of climate changes. for the society. In particular, there developed a significant interaction between senior scholars, junior scholars, PhD students, research students and master's students. Master's students from 12 European countries joined this session, which was organized byJ. Harff and P. Policastro. See the paper presented by P. Policastro, considering trans-national governance solutions: 'Climate Change and the Challenges for Law in Theory and Practice: A Proposal for the Baltic Region', which presented the conception of a Baltic IRIA (Inter-Regional Independent Authority). On the basis of this the students of the said European master's prepared a project of directive, with the title 'On the Realization of the United Nations Framework Convention on Climate Change' with the aim of protecting the existential manifestation of the person, nature and all other living creatures through the introduction of IRIAs (Framework Directive) (2010).

5 <https://www.rednetproject.eu/>.

of Pasquale Policastro, started the first steps in the creation of the platform 'Pensiero'. The aim of the platform is to develop an expert system, trying to take full advantage of the functions of law, regarding in particular new psychoactive substances, namely, prevention, supervision and sanction; the aim is to protect and enlarge the correct implementation of individual rights and freedoms. The fundamental role of lawyers in the development of such a system, involving different kinds of information and different kinds of knowledge, is to make sure that inputs and outputs of the expert system fully comply with constitutional values, in a national and a transnational perspective.

The interdisciplinary character of the activities related to the development of 'Pensiero' is still developing, due to the difficulty in fully accomplishing interdisciplinary research and applications. In terms of adaptation to the learning process, the difficulties in such a project sometimes go, in our understanding, beyond the outcomes representing the learning level – 'highly specialised knowledge, some of which is at the forefront of knowledge in a field of work or study' (Level 7 of European Qualification Framework). The methodological difficulties of this approach require, especially in the initial steps "knowledge advanced frontier at the [. . .] interface between fields", skills concerning "redefining [. . .] professional practice" together with a competence in 'sustained commitment' ranging at Level 8 of EQF. This made suitable the research of other activities as well, which may permit to support the level of application required for the 'Pensiero' platform. The importance of the latter platform of knowledge is, however, that its output is actually the development of a new legal specialization, suitable for the operation of an expert system, with special reference to telemedicine and/or action addressed to prevent the use of novel psychoactive substances.

The web application 'case-study creator' (see the next chapter by Nermend, Piwowarski and Policastro) appears to be a very interesting example, permitting the training and the development of knowledge, skills and competences of students at Levels 5-8 of the EQF. The extension of the platform to the needs of the legal professions would enhance very much the possibility of legal training to be developed, taking into account the true problems of the economic and social life. This would be very important, methodologically speaking, for the European Union in "modernising education and training systems, the interrelationship of education, training and employment and building bridges between formal, non-formal and informal learning, leading also to the validation of learning outcomes acquired through experience" (Recommendation of the European Parliament and of the Council of 23 April 2008, introduction [13]). It would help developing a European approach for European Education Area (see Bologna Declaration) consistent with the unicity of the project of the knowledge-based society.

Currently, we are undertaking activities that address the participation of students to the initiative of the African Union, called *La Grande Muraille Verte*,[6] within a project that we are elaborating which aims to inspire the development of synergies and initiatives in symbiosis with such a project. The initiative of the African Union involves eleven African countries, crossing Africa from Senegal to Djibouti. Its purpose is to create a band of trees 15 km wide and over 7,600 km long, covering a surface of over 11,600,000 ha. This endeavour would significantly contribute to the reconstruction of the biosphere. Therefore, in our belief, the contribution of the civil society to this project may be a road for a new approach to supranationality based upon values. The fundamental values related to it are peace and the reconstruction of biosphere. Whenever these values are achieved mainly through the active participation of the civil society, we would be in the presence of a new transnational approach to citizenship, going even beyond the borders of the European Union. The complexity of the project, which aims to involve around eleven States, tens of international organizations, bodies, hundreds of ministers and national agencies, tens of thousands of villages and inhabited centres, requires an approach sufficiently sophisticated and a cooperation of hundreds of NGO, think tanks and universities. For this reason we propose the development of a new approach to the web-based platform used for the case-study creator. This new approach aims to serve, by means of an expressly designed web platform (which we denoted as 'Joining Hands'), the more complex task of the coordination of the requests of intervention and the proposals of intervention in a project such as the Great Green Wall. Such an approach may permit European societies and societies of other continents to coordinate themselves to drive inspiration and develop synergies, while supporting African societies and institutions in all the tasks related to the full achievement of the project. Such tasks, starting from reforestation, include the related development of rural settlements, local economies, public services. Among such services we have energy production, transport, water distribution and, eventually, desalinization, as well as services to the enterprises. The significant interdisciplinary range of such needs shows, however, a remarkable importance of legal, administrative and political knowledge in the management of such coordination. Indeed, property, local governments, competition, trade, financial services, administrative law, international conventions, adjudication are some of the key elements that will be needed. The use of the platform Joining Hands, eventually coordinated at university level with sequences of dedicated Moodle facilities, including advanced related services, would permit the students of the different countries to intervene in the process of development of the Great Green Wall. It would permit them to interact with public authorities, civil servants, public and private managers, researchers,

6 A. Dia & R. Duponnois, *Le projet majeure africain de la Grande Muraille Verte. Concepts et mise en oeuvre*, Marseille, 2010.

university lecturers, creating transnational teams and groups. From the point of view of education, this variety of activities would serve to develop learning outcomes fit for Levels 6-8 of European Qualification Framework.[7] The platform Joining Hands, when applied to a significant project such as the Great Green Wall, may have as outcome the enlargement of the adoption of EQF beyond the European Union, with the consequent enlargement of the range of the knowledge-based society.

As a conclusion, we may say that a positive relation exists between the development of open research networks and the development of network-based forms of studies and legal training. This positive relation ought to be studied also by means of performance in terms of learning outcomes. However, the progress of innovation in the learning process is strictly related to innovation in research and its application, which leads to point out the central role of universities, not only as institutions but also as living parts of a new approach to civil society, with a strong transnational vocation.

7 Which, we remember, are, taking into account knowledge, skills and competence: Level 6 [**] – the learning outcomes relevant to Level 6 are advanced knowledge of a field of work or study, involving a critical understanding of theories and principles, advanced skills, demonstrating mastery and innovation, required to solve complex and unpredictable problems in a specialized field of work or study, management of complex technical or professional activities or projects, taking responsibility for decision-making in unpredictable work or study contexts and for managing professional development of individuals and groups.
Level 7 [***] – the learning outcomes relevant to Level 7 are highly specialized knowledge, some of which is at the forefront of knowledge in a field of work or study, as the basis for original thinking and/or research, critical awareness of knowledge issues in a field and at the interface between different fields, specialized problem-solving skills required in research and/or innovation in order to develop new knowledge and procedures and to integrate knowledge from different fields, management and transformation of work or study contexts that are complex, unpredictable and require new strategic approaches, responsibility for contributing to professional knowledge and practice and/or for reviewing the strategic performance of teams.
Level 8 [****] – the learning outcomes relevant to Level 8 are knowledge at the most advanced frontier of a field of work or study and at the interface between fields, the most advanced and specialized skills and techniques, including synthesis and evaluation, required to solve critical problems in research and/or innovation and to extend and redefine existing knowledge or professional practice, demonstration of substantial authority, innovation, autonomy, scholarly and professional integrity and sustained commitment to the development of new ideas or processes at the forefront of work or study contexts, including research.

13 The Szczecin Web Application 'Case-Study Creator' from Management to Legal Education and Training*

Kesra Nermend, Mateusz Piwowarski and Pasquale Policastro

13.1 Introduction

A constant and undisputed element that characterizes since ages the superior learning is to develop methods that are able to approach and solve a growing number of problems in a way that is clear, understandable and transmissible. One of the main problems that the present higher education faces is related to the extension of the methods and approaches of superior learning to wider groups of persons. This issue derives from the fact (well known to contemporary experience) that the time transformation of knowledge requires that any professional training is accustomed to approach new problems. In particular, for every professional it is demanded that creativity, modelling and problem-solving become a part of his or her own skills. Another problem is related to the development of the technological society, which requires that each professional field of interest may be adequately aware of its interface with other disciplines. It is also for this reason that we see new scientific approaches, such as compliance, which nowadays join mainly decision-making in the enterprises with legal knowledge. However, the dynamic character of the different sciences requires the development of a growing mutual link. Law, in particular, which is called to regulate an unlimited number of issues, requires to devote a special interest to this issue. For this reason the purpose of this short article will be to highlight how a platform explicitly designed to support the co-operation between universities and companies may be extended to legal activities as a tool to permit the compliance between societal needs concerning law and the capabilities of the legal professions. In this sense we may also extend compliance approach to the methods addressed to confront undertakings working within the societies with the learning process. In this way we may conceive a meta-dimension of compliance itself, related to learning.

* Although the chapter is the result of a close cooperation between the authors, it was Kesra Nermed who developed the conception of the application case-study generator, Mateusz Piwowarski developed its description, and Pasquale Policastro conceived the adaptation of the model to innovation in legal education.

Starting from the Polish example, the general task of the contemporary higher education is addressed to enhance research attitude, obtain professional knowledge, and enhance problem-solving and entrepreneurial attitude.[1] When dealing with law, this statement seems clearly addressed not to neglect jurisprudence and theoretical knowledge while developing learning in an environment that appears close to the professional life. The third element of the above-mentioned statement appears instead related to the organization framework of the legal profession and addressed the development of law firms in the conditions to develop and to follow the needs of the market. In this perspective there shows a significant analogy between legal studies, legal training and the world of management. Furthermore, according to the strategical document Europa 2020,[2] as well as the Regional Innovation Strategies,[3] among the tasks of higher education, we also have to develop a platform of dialogue between universities and the enterprises. Such a dialogue shall result in the increase in the chances of the students obtaining an employment after their studies consistent with the professional profile developed through the education received. It shall also result in an enhancement of the role of education in the triangle of knowledge, connecting education, research and innovation.

Considering management, the poor cooperation between enterprises and the research centres, including universities in Poland, is shown also in the survey 'Barriers to the cooperation between the enterprises and the research centers',[4] which was developed in 2006 by the Polish Ministry of Science and Higher Education. Its main results show the need to increase the awareness of the possibility to cooperate between companies and institutes of higher education. They also show the need to make clear the range of possible cooperation. As the survey shows, for every five companies in Poland, one does not even know of the possibility of such cooperation, and for every two companies interested to cooperate, one does not know how to reach the relative higher education institute or centre of research. Another important question concerns the active role of the scholars and the researchers in such a process. Indeed, almost half of the surveyed enterprises declared that they became aware of the possibilities to cooperate with higher education or research institutes following the initiative of some of the scholars or researchers. However, the 33% of the companies that do not cooperate with universities or higher

1 See, for example, the debate on the social competencies as an outcome of higher education in Poland. M. Novak-Dziemianowicz, 'Kompetencje społenczne jako jeden z efektów kształcenia w krajowych ramach kwalifikacji w kontekście pytań o cele i funkcji edukacji', Instytut Badań Edukacyjnych, Warszawa 2001, pp. 19-20.

2 European Commission 'EUROPA 2020', Bruxelles, 2010.

3 "A Regional Innovation Strategy (RIS) is a document created in each region (*voivodship*) in co-operation with representatives of educational institutions, regional authorities, organizations uniting entrepreneurs and business related institutions [. . .] The main task of the strategy is to specify the ways of increasing innovativeness in the region." See the Polish Innovation Portal: <www.pi.gov.pl/eng/chapter_86528.asp>.

4 'Bariery współpracy przedsiębiorców i ośrodków naukowych', Ministerstwo Nauki i Szkolnictwa Wyższego, Departament Wdrożeń i Innowacji, Bariery współpracy przedsiębiorców i ośrodków naukowych, Warszawa, 2006.

education institutes claim that they did not receive relative offers of cooperation from their side.

The expectations of the students show that the existing flow of exchanges between the world of enterprises and the world of higher education is far from being satisfactory. Indeed, according to the survey of the Polish Agency for the Development of Entrepreneurship[5] concerning academic entrepreneurship (2009), the learning method given by the intensive forms of learning based upon the cases meets both consensus and proves, in the cases where it is applied, to be efficient.

Using the method of the case study was made possible through the intensification of the cooperation between higher education institutions, including students, researchers, senior scholars and professors. We would like here to point out how this approach is important for the legal training. Indeed, it is only when legal education takes place with a strong emphasis on the problems of the real world, and on the practical skills required together with knowledge, that there is no risk of a discontinuity between learning at the university or at the law school, and the learning within the legal corporation or the magistracy. Such a discontinuity may pose a risk for the proper transfer of both legal knowledge and, in some cases, the ethical standards. For this reason the practice of the faculties of the schools of economics and management and the practice of the law faculties ought to develop in parallel paths.

13.2 THE PROBLEM OF COOPERATION BETWEEN COMPANIES AND UNIVERSITIES

We may also see at the regional level the scale and the quality of the problems connected, from on the one hand, with the insufficient use by the companies of the potential provided by scientific research and academic knowledge, and, on the other hand, with the insufficient use of practical experience of the enterprises in the learning process. As we had the occasion to underline such a problem, when considered at the regional level, it may lead to a growing discouragement: (1) for the graduates of the local universities to undertake their activity with success; (2) in the degree of innovation of the local enterprises and in their weakness, with respect to conjuncture; (3) with the difficulties of the consulting companies and the law firms to take a dimension which ranges beyond the local activities, with a consequent shrinking of the market for the services; (4) and, as a consequence, to the final decision of the potential students to study outside the region.[6] For what concerns the surveys on the field, a project called 'Innovative teaching as an opportunity to reinforce the cooperation

5 Polska Agenca Rozwoju Przedsiębiorczości (PARP).

6 P. Policastro, 'Innovation', Keynote speech at the Polish IT society annual conference, Międzyzdroje 22 September 2012.

between enterprises and the scientific sector',[7] permitted to develop, among other things, field analyses.

From the perspective of the teachers, the majority of them (68%) observed that they lack access to adequate innovative tools fit for the needs of the students. Furthermore, 82% of the academic teachers said that they have only a limited opportunity to transmit their knowledge in a way which may be both innovative and attractive for the students. When asked to explain in detail their point, the teachers referred to the need to work out viable didactic tools which may (1) motivate the students to actively participate in their courses and (2) permit students to organize their work in the classes and at home, for example, permitting the students to work in small groups, orienting their activity to specific tasks.

From the perspective of the enterprises, 100% of the firms which participated in the survey consider the possibility of cooperating with the university as an opportunity. Such an interest, however, appears related not only to management aspects but to technological, financial and legal aspects.

From the perspective of the university, the development of tools which may permit such a wider cooperation is especially important since its prestige may significantly increase. In this framework, the 'creator of the case study' was developed.

13.3 The Creator of Case Study

13.3.1 The Tool and Its Users

The proposed tool is a new form of cooperation of the business world with the world of science, based upon the use of a computer-based platform of communication in the process of solving real and present problems, which may occur in the economic activity. Among the most important aspects concerning such communication, the following have been considered:

1. the possibility for the enterprises to properly present their problems to the academic community, in order to have them solved;
2. the adequate solution to the presented problems by the academic teachers through the case study;

7 This project has been realized through a contract between a company belonging to Szczecin University, the Centrum Transferu Wiedzy i Technologii Uniwersytetu Szczecińskiego Sp. z o.o (Centre for the Transfer of Knowledge and Technology of Szczecin University Ltd.), and the Region of West Pomerania together with the Regional Labour Office, contract no. UDA-PO KL.08.01.02-32-017/11.

3. the presentation of the case study to the students to permit them to get to know how to solve a problem presented by an enterprise;
4. the establishment of contacts between the researchers and the academic teachers.

The users of the creator of case study are four main typologies of subjects:

1. the enterprises, which present the problems to solve, monitor the developments in the processing of their requests via the platform and, once the case study is solved, obtain the solution, eventually participating in its discussion and analysis
2. the academic teachers and the researchers, who may survey the problems as they are presented by the firms and decide to develop them into a case, finding a suitable solution and presenting it on the platform, enriching it with further elements following feedbacks from the companies and the academic environment
3. the students, who may look at the case studies
4. the administrator, as an auxiliary subject with full privileges and the task to manage the users

The creator of the case study is developed as an Internet application, which may be accessed from any place, at any time, through a web browser, and deals with the interaction of the following functions performed by the different groups of subjects (Table 13.1):

Table 13.1 Subjects and Functions

Entrepreneur	Lecturer	Students	Administrator
Logs in	Logs in	Logs in	Logs in
Edits user profile	Edits user profile	Edits user profile	Surveys
Exposes a problem with a request of solution	Looks at the problems presented	–	Distributes problems
Checks for the status of the request	Creates and edits the case study	Looks at the case study	Edits distribution
Edits the exposition	Surveys case studies	Looks at the case study	Manages users
Looks at the case study	Contacts with the firms	–	Has full control of all the functions, manages the users

13.3.2 The Architecture of the Case-Study Creator

The case-study creator is based upon the classical architecture Model-View-Control (MVC): the "framework exists to separate the representation of information from user interaction", and is based upon a vision "to capture the end user cognitive model of roles and interactions between them".[8] It is structured in three layers:[9]

1. The model, which represents the set of information on which the application operates – in this case the model addresses business logic.
2. The view, which transforms the modelled information in a web page suited to interact with the users.
3. The controller, which reacts on the action of the user and manages suitable changes in the layer of the model or the view.

The architecture of the application following the MVC scheme is represented in Figure 13.1:

Figure 13.1 Architecture WWW of the Application Case-Study Creator

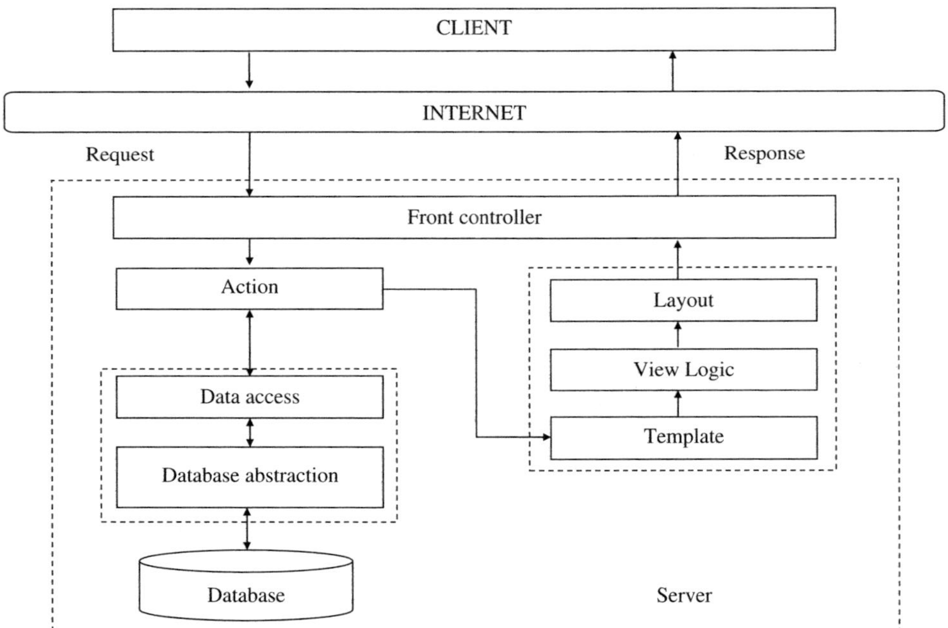

Source: Elaboration on the ground of 'The Definitive Guide to Symphony'.[10]

8 T. Reenskaug & J.O. Coplien, *The DCI Architecture: A New Vision of Object-Oriented Programming*, 20 March 2009. *See* <www.artima.com/articles/dci_vision.html>.

9 Włodzimierz Gajda, *PHP, MySQL i MVC. Tworzenie witryn WWW opartych na bazie danych*, Helion, 2010.

10 F. Zaninotto & F. Potencier, *The Definitive Guide to Symfony*, Apress, Berkeley, CA, 2007.

The project framework of MCV is characterized by a separation of the model of the date, user interface and the logic organized in such a way that the modification to one part may influence the other parts in a minimal measure. The fundamental idea of the MVC is to structure the application into parts, a user interface easy to modify and different modalities of presentation. In the construction of the case-study creator all the capabilities of the MVC approach have been consequently used and implemented.

13.3.3 The Functional Architecture of the Case-Study Creator

The access to the functionality of the creator is possible after creating an account, registering in the system and undergoing the process of authorization of the users. The main function of the creator is presented in Figure 13.2.

Each of the users, during the process of registration, introduces some basic information, name and address, which can be modified at any time from the level of the panel of the

Figure 13.2 Functional Architecture of the Creator of the Case Study

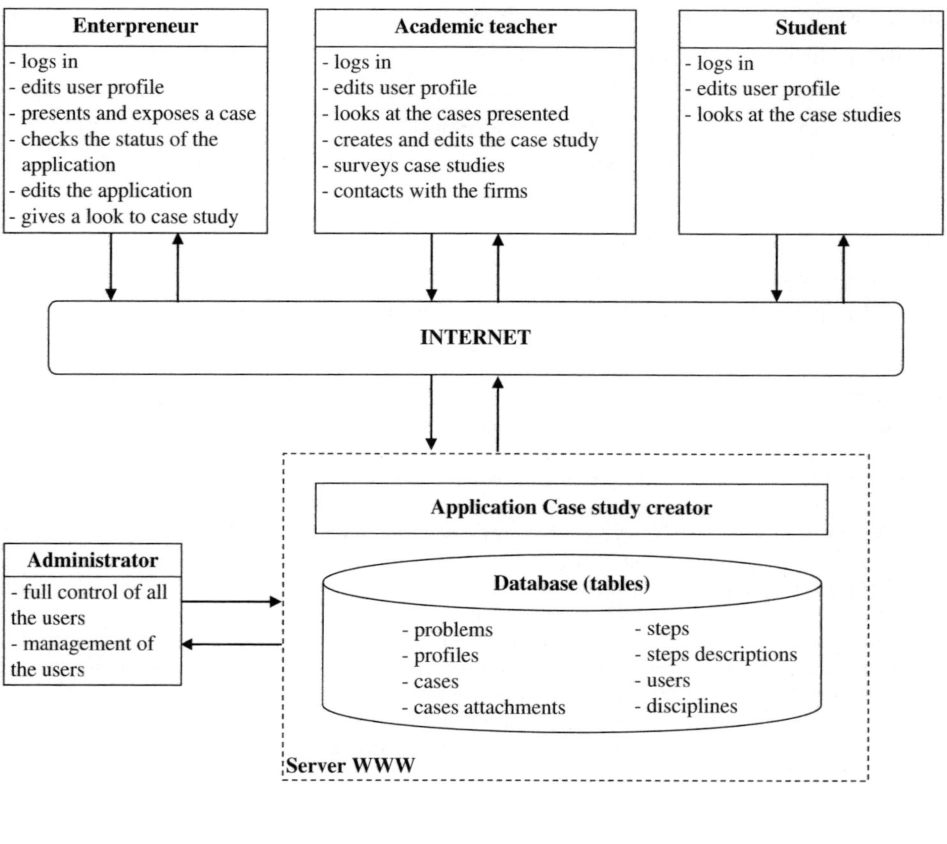

user. The company, which aims to receive knowledge-based support from the academic community, has the possibility to present a problem to solve. For this purpose the company needs to fill a form and may append files that describe the question in detail, entering everything in the platform. The academic teachers and researchers, who have access to the problems presented, may take them up them to find solutions. The solved problems are presented in the form of a worked-out case study.

The creator enables to make and look at a case study in the form of a process organized in a flow of several steps according to the methodology of its creation. The structure of the case study includes eleven steps at this stage, but the researcher or the academic teacher, at the time when the architecture is defined, may resign from some of its elements. Among such steps, we have the following, for the strictly management-based application: introduction, the aim, the summary, the environment of the object, the problem, the main actors and their role, the risk of the problem, the variants of the solution to the problem, the SWOT/PEST[11] analysis, the summary and other information included in the case study as annexes. At every step of the creation (modification) there is the possibility to add a free quantity of information, in text form and graphic form. The use of the Creator is made easy by different hints. During the process of creation and of the confirmation of the case study on the system, the enterprise is properly informed. The user can look at the case study in those steps by means of which the case study has been created. There is also the possibility to generate a case study as a unitary document in pdf format. The students, after the registration in the system, may profit from the developed solutions. The students may, however, access only the cases that concern their discipline of studies/field of specialization.

The creator of the case study permits, however, a wider development of the contact between the academic world and the enterprises. It is also for this reason that the possibility of extending the platform may be of significant importance.

11 The SWOT analysis is accounted for Albert S. Humphrey, and is an approach for evaluating a business. Therefore it is an analysis of the micro-environment. It was developed in the years 1960-1970 at the Stanford Research Institute (now SRI International). It is based upon the establishment of the following elements relating good and bad with present and future: (1) whether an operation is Satisfactory (Strengths) at present, (2) whether an operation gives Opportunities for the future, (3) what are the Weaknesses (Faults) of the operation at present, (4) what are the Threats for the future. So it may be looked in two perspectives: A. Good: Present-Future, B. Bad: Present-Future (SOFT), or I. Present: Good-Bad, II. Future: Good-Bad (SWOT). See the seminal contribution of A. Humphrey in SRI Alumni Association Newsletter, December 2005, <www.sri.com/about/alumni/alumni-newletters>.
For PEST (PESTEL analysis), *see* instead A. Gillespie, *Foundations of Economics*, 2nd edn, additional chapter on Business Strategy, Oxford University Press online resources, in particular <www.oup.com/uk/orc/bin/9780199296378/01student/additional/page_12.htm>, where such analysis is presented as an analysis of the macro-environment and includes the factors that affect business decisions. We have the following relevant factors: Political, Economic, Social, Technological, Environmental, Legal. From this we derive the abbreviation PEST, which may be enlarged to PESTEL.

13.4 The Use and the Extension of the Platform

13.4.1 The Problem of Use Taking into Account the Different Aspects Related to the Creation of the Application

The contact with the enterprises makes it possible to increase the quality of approach to teaching, collecting interesting problems derived from the practice. Such problems, according to their difficulty and the state of affairs, may be solved during the study classes or through writing the works or the dissertations demanded at the end of the different cycles of studies, including, in the most complex cases, dedicated PhD dissertations. In all these events, the relation between the companies and the university, and especially the researchers, the academic teachers and the managers of the companies, not only improves in quality but permits to include to a growing extent the students. Indeed, the students, working under the supervision of their teachers and professors, have the possibility to get to know the most recent issues concerning the life of the companies, and develop their knowledge in continuity with the experience of the companies, thus acquiring important knowledge based upon application. This means non only a better training for the students but also a growing worth of the knowledge gained by the students for the companies. The companies, from their side, acquire the possibility to be informed and make use of the most recent advances and state-of-the-art knowledge for their purposes.

13.4.2 Legal Questions and the Development of the Case-Study Creator

The extension of the platform given by the application to legal questions seems to be extremely important both for the internal development of the case-study creator and for its extension as a method to improve, by means of a virtual and coordinated space, the connection between demand and offer; therefore the importance of extending the platform is connected to the fact that it makes the services it deals with more efficient.

13.4.3 Legal Questions and the Development of the Platform

However, the study of the environment of the project shows that the platform has been developed mainly for regional approaches, on the one hand, and for merely educational approaches, on the other. The development of the platform requires to take into explicit account in its architecture the fact that information received and transmitted are related to companies, which may compete. Therefore, treatment of the data as an anonymous presentation of the case includes a double form of presenting the outcomes of the case study: one tailored for the companies that present some problems on the platform, and another tailored as a case, which may be accessible to the student without disclosing reserved information or any other information that may be used by the competitors. To find answers to these problems, we need not only to develop the architecture of the system but also to consider the legal issues related to it. Indeed, a very important problem is whether the approach made through the platform ought to be considered as an example, which other universities may follow, targeting a limited number of companies, or in case of the case-study generator, it may be expanded following a path similar to other web-based portals. The question is of some importance, since the case-study generator permits to access advice of a comparatively high level with respect to the ordinary market conditions, at a relatively competitive cost. This aspect would benefit the universities, which may gradually introduce their students into the practice of their profession, supporting at the same time the freedom of circulation of services on a European and global scale, with an increase in the overall efficiency of the related markets.

13.4.4 The Extension of the Platform to the Legal Profession

The importance of the development of the platform is related also to its use for what concerns law, as well as other more targeted activities in relation to different professional abilities, such as purposes that address common good.

For what concerns law specificallyl, the development of the application the companies that are addressing their requests to the case-study creator, may be very well informed of the possibility to ask also for legal help. In particular, the company may address all the questions concerning the legal compliance. The application, with its integrated possibility to develop SWOT/PESTEL analysis, requires joint interdisciplinary resources. The questions of compliance are of growing importance for the companies, and they intermingle with many fields of law. Neglecting such questions may indeed cause huge costs for the firm, losses in market shares and fines (for example, when the company neglects to comply with European competition law).

However, together with the questions related to compliance, there are many other questions that require legal advice and counsel. Here the platform developed for the case-study creator assumes an autonomous importance for legal profession, with motivations, however, which go beyond the reasons that justify the case-study creator. Indeed, the case-study creator has been developed for the main reason to join companies based in the region with the university, creating thus a virtuous circle of quality of learning-companies' development-employment-innovation, centred on the regional environment.

Legal profession has the complementary priority to go beyond regional boundaries, to avoid too tight a competition between local law firms, their fragmentation and the subsequent impossibility for the firms to follow the demand of the market. Indeed, today only a law firm with a significant portfolio of clients and enough of practitioners may offer knowledge and capabilities for the demand of European economy.

What is important is that when the regional environment of the legal firms is not in itself based upon big and internationally developed firms, the skills of the lawyers to work in bigger groups of structured specialization shall be taught at the university. The teaching of such skills may not take place but by practice, by learning by doing.

The importance of such an approach has a general meaning for all the legal professions. For the students of law who wish to accede to the judicial career, the interplay between the dynamics of the judicial affairs and processes of legal, political and economic integration, which take place within or beyond the will of the states, requires an adequate training. Such training shall be based upon adequate tools. Also for the legal professions related to court administration, or that address the public function or administration affairs at large, the importance to go beyond the present horizons of the profession is related to the general need for a university training, which trains professionals, who may excel and take the lead in the dynamic state of affairs of their interest.

For this reason, the importance of a training based upon an adequate interaction between the dynamic world of business and of the legal profession demands for a wider application of e-based platforms. The extension of the case-study creator to uses related to legal profession has been developed so far through experimental forms of interaction as well as through a designing and initial implementation of didactic process, involving law students[12] or addressing projects that fit the purpose.[13] The students seem to be happy, and for the university this paves the way for higher quality in the compliance with the learning standards.

12 Such activities join the students of management with the students of Law of the European Master in Law and Policies of European Integration: European Constitutional Law and Multilevel Constitutionalism (master's studies in partnership between University Autonoma of Barcelona, University of Milan I, University of Montpellier I, Szczecin University) and are addressed to test the case-study creator.

13 Such as the project The Great Green Wall Synergy, Symbiosis & Inspiration, which is based upon a platform similar to the case-study creator, the architecture of which is generated starting from the developments of the Moodle Platform which supports the seminar on Constitutional Law of the Biosphere and the Great Green Wall at Szczecin University.

14 Artificial Intelligence Application to Legal Studies and Training of Legal Professions: Some Reflections for a Syllabus

Pasquale Policastro, Agata Wawrzyniak and Barbara Wąsikowska

This article starts from a debate that began in 2005 and addressed improvements in the level of legal training, joining it with research and a wider understanding of legal professions. The first parts of the debate concerned the article published by Paolo Nunziante on the 'Legal Semiosphere' in 2005.[1] The said article was aimed at showing the crossroads between theoretical reflection and application of an advanced cybernetic paradigm for the treatment of language. Such an approach would have had in turn important applicative consequences, leading to a 'predictive' paradigm of law and development of a new legal profession, the 'legal analyst' serving the application of artificial intelligence (AI) methods to law. The article led to debates and seminars, which started between Emilio Castorina, Teresa Freixes, Paolo Nunziante, Otto Pfersmann, and Pasquale Policastro, within the PhD seminars provided by the latter at the University of Salerno in the period 2005-2008[2] and at the ECONET[3] school held in Ragusa on 19 April 2008 on 'Language and Constitution: a Key Issue for European Integration'. The reflections led to the development of scientific considerations,[4] as well as their implementation in the curricula of

1 P. Nunziante, La Semiosfera giuridica, in Innovazione e Diritto – n. 1-2/2005, pp. 3-11. See also the presentation of the journal by R. Perrone Capano, where he envisaged the development of a "multilingual project, which, in cooperation with the foundation OPENLAB, has as its objective to experiment new models of artificial intelligence supporting the translation of legal texts from Italian to main community languages and vice versa".

2 'Return of the Brains' grant of Italian Ministry of Instruction, University and Research (MIUR), by Pasquale Policastro, at the University of Salerno in the years 2005-2008 dedicated to "The transformation of the system of the legal sources of European constitutional law: paradigms of constitutionalism, fundamental principles and methods of knowledge and interpretation".

3 Centre of Research and Advanced Training in European Constitutional Law.

4 E. Castorina, 'Constitutional Language and European Integration', *in* E. Castorina & P. Policastro, *Liberty and Language. The Global Dimension of European Constitutional Integration*, Torino, 2011, pp. 111-129; among the relevant position in the latter collection, we have: P. Policastro, 'Constitutionalism, Comparison, Complexity: Prolegomena on Liberty and the Use of Language for a Predictive Theory of Law', pp. 15-109; we also have T. Freixes, 'La igualdad de mujeres y hombres en el Derecho de la Unión Europea. Una valoración tras la entrada en vigor del Tratado de Lisboa', pp. 369-365.

studies, with a clear attempt to give a practical and applicative dimension to legal training. Therefore, the European Master in Law and Policies of European Integration: European Constitutional Law and Multilevel Constitutionalism included the results of the debate into its curriculum. Indeed, a section of Module 11 of the master's (Economy of European Integration and Technological Societies) has been dedicated to methodology of the legal knowledge and AI.[5]

The attention shown on the subject was also motivated from the interest to attain a growing integration between the research provided by the different partners of the master's[6] and the research developed by the students of the master's. The first attempt to define a common research topic was the project 'EUROGLOS – A Multicultural Glossary of European Constitutional Law and of the Constitutional Developments in the Neighbouring Regions'. The project, for which an adequate frame of cooperation is yet to be developed, led, however, to essential methodological reflections.[7] A second project, which led to an important reflection on how to join, through AI, different disciplines, has been the ReDNet project, coordinated by the University of Hertfordshire.[8]

A significant impulse towards the development of an interdisciplinary syllabus joining Artificial Intelligence with Technological Society has been given by the development of the project 'Menu for Justice – Toward a European Curriculum Studiorum on Judicial Studies'. Indeed, both in the different activities of the task forces and in the debates disseminating the project, the issues of the 'interdisciplinary' evolution of the curricula of legal studies and training had a meaningful role. This reinforced the conviction that further developments of the European Master in Law and Policies of European Integration: European Constitutional Law and Multilevel Constitutionalism should continue in the

5 The first cycle of lessons was given by Paolo Nunziante.

6 All together the full partners, associated partners and cooperating partners are as follows: the Autonomous University of Barcelona, State University of Milan, University of Montpellier I, Szczecin University, University of Turin, National University for Distance Learning (UNED – Spain), University of Essex, University of Barcelona, University HUB-KU Bruxelles, University of Cambridge (UK), FOM Munich, Hochschule Munich, University of Lapland, Marmara University of Istanbul, Moscow State University of International Relations (MGIMO), Warsaw University, Polish Academy of Sciences, University of Wrocław, University of Paris I, University of Regensburg, University of Minho (Portugal), University of Hertfordshire, University of Lisbon.

7 *See* the 'comparative sieve' by P. Policastro in the appendix to 'Constitutionalism, Comparison, Complexity: Prolegomena on Liberty and the Use of Language for a Predictive Theory of Law', *in* E. Castorina & P. Policastro, *Liberty and Language. The Global Dimension of European Constitutional Integration*, Torino, 2011, pp. 94-109. The title of the appendix is "A project of comparative sieve as a learning tool for constitutional law in a multilingual context. [. . .] ECONET – European Multicultural Glossary of Constitutional Law – Euroglos.

8 K. Bogusławski, O. Corazza & P. Policastro, *Legal Training and Legal Profession at the Crossroad with Pharmacology and Telemedicine: Designing a System for Preventing the Circulation of New Psychoactive Substances* (see *infra*).

field of an interdisciplinary approach. Here we would like to point out that the search for interdisciplinary subjects, such as AI, is especially important since it is a powerful 'language' permitting to communicate different sciences. Therefore, starting from 2010, a growing number of interdisciplinary activities were proposed to the students of the said master's; these activities involved reflection on ethical and Islamic banking, constitutional issues on climate change, transfer of technology from enterprises to university, opportunities and ethical issues raised by nanotechnologies, etc. Furthermore, to define some basic questions on the interdisciplinary evolution of the master's studies and the integration between legal training and interdisciplinary research, between November 2011 and November 2012, a number of seminars were developed on 'Interdisciplinary methods in legal modelling and learning process', which were held at the Faculty of Law and Administration and at the Faculty of Economics and Management of Szczecin University, as well as at the Academic Information Centre of Szczecin University. These seminars, coordinated by Pasquale Policastro, saw the participation of Kesra Nermend, Krzysztof Bogusławski, Małgorzata Łatusińska, Barbara Królikowska, Barbara Wąsikowska, Agata Wawrzyniak, Ille Gebeshuber and Teresa Freixes.[9] These seminars were largely inspired by the 'interdisciplinary law modelling' regarding different kind of problems, which were related to treat, for the purpose of legal analysis, data stemming from different disciplines, each one having a different horizon of investigation and a different object of application.[10]

After justifying with some more reflection the importance of studying Artificial Intelligence in the frame of the Technological Society, we will discuss a syllabus of a module devoted to Artificial Intelligence and Technological Society, which may lead to further innovation in legal education.

For what concerns the use of AI methods in legal education, the aim of the module would not be to teach AI as such. It would rather be introducing its main methods and their application in a way understandable and useful to the lawyers. The making of the syllabus should take the moves from the fact that the aim of the studies, for which universities and lecturers are accounted for, is to permit the students to acquire knowledge, skills and competences.[11] We have, in this perspective, to take into account that the interdisciplinary

9 The latter from the Technical University of Vienna, on leave of absence at Institute of Microengineering and Nanoelectronics (IMEN) of the National University of Malaysia.

10 P. Policastro, 'Constitutionalism vs. Economic Analysis: On the Use of Founding Theories and Complementary Theories in Constitutional Interpretation', *in* S. Kirste, A. van Aaken, M. Anderheiden & P. Policastro (Eds.), *Interdisciplinary Research in Jurisprudence and Constitutionalism: Archiv für Rechts- und Sozialphilosophie*, Vol. 1, 2012; ibid., keynote speech, Budapest, 2012.

11 Recommendation of the European Parliament and of the Council of 23 April 2008 on the establishment of the European Qualifications Framework for lifelong learning, introduction (1).

purpose to create knowledge goes beyond the assumptions and the aims we set for each science. Multidisciplinary approaches consider instead some parallel development of knowledge, which is deemed to converge.[12] Indeed, we have to take into account that the development of knowledge, skills and competences in some specific studies, such as legal studies, goes parallel with the learning processes in other fields, such as the management studies, economical studies and information studies. The augmentation of the quality of each of the studies in question goes together with the development of an awareness going beyond each of these fields. There are indeed possibilities to gain knowledge, improve the skills and enlarge competences making use of other methods as well. However, "the more the number of variables we aim to isolate and to control in our theory, the more we wish to take into account auxiliary theories with respect to our object, the more the theory attains a higher level to complexity. This is due to manifold relations existing between the object or the target of the enquiry and the purposes of the observer, who is at the same time inquiring, theorizing, creating and developing relations among the variable elements, and then executing the interpretation 'models' into practice in order to attain his/her purposes".[13]

The augmentation of knowledge, skills and competencies, therefore, is a process that goes together with (1) the whole process of learning of a given person and (2) processes of learning together. This perspective relates to two questions, connected to interdisciplinary research and learning: (a) How much does an individual who is following a study in a discipline, such as law, need to study another discipline, such as AI, to be able to make use of it in developing his or her skills? (b) How much the students from other fields, which may be considered as useful for law, but are different from it, shall study law to be able to communicate with a lawyer? If we approach this problem only taking into account the question of information, which is knowledge in the form of methods and notionspotentially to be put into practice, the question may have a limited range of interest. We may conclude that since a subject such as AI may have only a limited meaning for the essence of legal training, it may only have a limited purpose to enlarge the horizons of the student.

The approach to higher education in terms of achievements of a coordinated level of knowledge, skills and competences calls us instead to consider that we need to develop,

12 Ray J. Solomonoff, *Three Kinds of Probabilistic Induction: Universal Distributions and Convergence Theorems*, London, 2003. The problem of the universal distribution and convergence, developed by Solomonoff and, in a somehow parallel way, by A.N. Kolmogorov, takes into account what it appears to be the overall spectrum of machine learning, and at the same time, presents the possibility of getting to join theoretical knowledge with applicative one, including the competence for applicative purposes.

13 Policastro 2012, pp. 173-174.

within the curricula of studies, the possibility to put the knowledge into practice and implement such knowledge in reality. For this reason, in the technological society, it is worth considering that all the aspects of human culture are at crossroads between many disciplines, such as law, economics, medicine, biology, technology, information science and others.

The first lessons of a module should therefore explain what can be solved through AI and why the methods of AI came into existence. On this basis, the presentation of the general features of the module shall motivate the student to devote energy to issues that are at the "forefront of knowledge" and are at the same time at "the interface between different fields".[14] AI is indeed a discipline that presents a significant application range, which joins information technology (IT) with other fields of science and knowledge.[15] In the latest years, the increase of computational power, the growth in the amount of available data and the necessity to approach the problems taking into account their systemic features led to a dynamic development of AI as a science, as well as in its application. The essence of systems based on AI is the possibility of processing data expressed in a numeric, binary form as well as in a linguistic, logical one. Since these data can also consist of ordered sequences of elements or tables and contain elements described in a very imprecise or even subjective way,[16] it is important to present to the students the applications first and the possibilities that are available for them to improve their knowledge, professional skills and competences by means of such methods. An important element is to show, at the beginning of the syllabus, the existence in the university, or in connected agendas, of approaches addressed to make use of these methods.[17]

The second part of the introductory lessons ought to deal with AI as an opportunity to solve problems that could not be solved by other, formerly adopted approaches. Such a section shall also include some basic examples. Indeed, the use of data required, first, a qualitative transformation in the knowledge of the processes related to understanding and

---

14 *See* Recommendation of the European Parliament and of the Council of 23 April 2008 on the establishment of the European Qualifications Framework for lifelong learning, Annex II, Descriptors defining levels in the European Qualifications Framework (EQF), Level 7.

15 The importance of these approaches for applications in the field of legal studies may be seen, for example, in some important contributions of some years ago: S. Hoa Nguyen, J.G. Bazan, A. Skowron & H. Son Nguyen, 'Layered Learning for Concept Synthesis', *in* J.F. Peters *et al.* (Eds.), *Transactions on Rough Sets I*, Lecture Notes in Computer Science, Springer, Berlin, 2004, pp. 187-208; R.S. Milton, V. Uma Maheshvari & A. Siromoney, *Rough Sets and Relational Learning*, pp. 321-337.

16 L. Rutkowski, *Metody i techniki sztucznej inteligencji*, PWN, Warszawa, 2005.

17 For a consideration of the platform PENSIERO, see Legal Training and Legal Profession at the Crossroad with Pharmacology and Telemedicine: Designing a System for Preventing the Circulation of New Psychoactive Substances; the development of the platform EUROGLOS also appears to be a significant example.

modelling reality. Indeed, notwithstanding the power of their tools, the methods based on conventional mathematics were not able to deal with making use of verbal information until recent days. However, not taking the said information into consideration highly confined efficacy and effectiveness of different methods of modelling, forecasting, designing, steering, etc. These aspects shall be cleared with some examples; for instance, voting behaviour, labour law negotiations, decision-making underlining the opportunity of making use of new methods, which would permit using this type of information as well.[18]

To complete the introduction, a brief presentation on how AI method came into existence may give a scale of the importance of the phenomenon. Indeed, the researches which led to the development of the artificial intelligence approaches, were started to be developed on a significant scale since the end of the 1950s and the 1960s, and contributed to the development of a new branch of science, the so-called computational intelligence. Elaborate first algorithms of learning machines were the predecessors of contemporary neural nets. Subsequently, in the 1970s the bases of fuzzy sets theory and fuzzy logic were created. Intensive studies were also conducted on the development of genetic algorithms. In the beginning of the 1980s the bases of representation of knowledge founded upon rough sets theory were created as well. In the recent years many hybrid methods were developed which join learning systems with evolutionary and fuzzy systems.[19]

Looking at the development of computational intelligence, we may see that there developed two main approaches: one is related to the development of cognitive sciences, while the other is related to the development of engineering sciences. This section of the module will explain the importance of such modelling and tools and their foundation, as considered within an approach to legal theory and practice.

The core of the module should be devoted to the possible application of AI in law. Indeed, one of the first of them was medicine, and was later followed by many applications into economy, bioinformatics, robotics, logistics and even music and art.[20] For law, the treatment of natural language is of paramount importance. While studying law, the student is frequently forced to search legal databases in order to find appropriate legal acts, legal norms or other relevant data. Legal databases contain information about facts which have

18 *See* Z. Pawlak, 'Some Issues on Rough Sets', *in* J.F. Peters *et al.* (Eds.), *Transactions on Rough Sets I*, Springer, Berlin, 2004, pp. 1-58. A number of applications have been worked out indeed for other business applications as well, *e.g.* small company income, product quality, *etc. See* A. Piegat, *Zastosowania zbiorów przybliżonych w ekonomii, lectures* – copied manuscript, Uniwersytet Szczeciński, Szczecin, 2005/2006.

19 Piegat 2005/2006; Rutkowski 2005.

20 For what concerns music, *see* A. Czyżewski, M. Szczerbka & B. Kostek, Musical Phrase Representation and Recognition by Means of Neural Networks and Rough Sets, *in* Peters 2004, pp. 254-278.

or may have legal meaning or information included in legal acts texts, legal interpretation texts and legal doctrine. There obviously exist special information-searching systems. However, it often happens that despite applying appropriate key words according to which the database has to be searched, the information obtained as a result of searching is incorrect or not on the subject. This is the reason that justifies the presentation of different methods of natural language analysis as well as the newest advances. Indeed, the present reality demands to deal with different languages and legal cultures at the same time. This is the main problem of comparative law, namely, dealing not only with different cultures but also with their mutual interaction.

To illustrate the development of approaches to translation may be a very good starting point for the overall understanding of what the tasks are and the potential for the application of AI methods. Indeed, a discipline called computational linguistics, which deals with computer application for studying natural languages, appeared shortly after building the first computers by the end of 1940s. Even though the first programmes for language analysis appeared in 1960s,[21] the approach to machine translation by means of programmes appears in many aspects problematic. Indeed, even the most recent systems work correctly only in narrow scientific fields. For this reason, the treatment of natural language may seem to require more advanced approaches, going much beyond statistically based approaches or the attempts of formalizing internal rules of language.[22] Inductive approaches to knowledge, which lead to the use of neural networks, appear more interesting.[23] However, before approaching neural networks, particularly useful can be an analysis of rough sets theory. Started by Zdzisław Pawlak in 1980s and developed for a number of years by its inventor and many other researchers, it is a theoretical basis of various IT methods and tools that allow among others decision-making rules induction or data sets reduction.[24] Rough sets theory became highly popular and is currently used for data mining and

21 Y. Bar-Hillel, 'The Present Status of Automatic Translation of Languages', *Advances in Computers*, Vol. 1, 1960, pp. 91-163.

22 J. Bateman, 'Upper Modeling: Organizing Knowledge for Natural Language Processing', Proc. Fifth International Workshop on Natural Language Generation, Pittsburgh, PA, 1990.

23 R. Solomonoff, *The Mechanization of Linguistic Learning*, Second International Congress on Cybernetics, 1958, pp. 180-193; R. Solomonoff, *A New Method for Discovering the Grammars of Phrase Structure Languages, Information Processing*, UNESCO, Paris, 1960.

24 Among the different works, *see* A. Mrózek & L. Płonka, *Analiza danych metodą zbiorów przybliżonych. Zastosowania w ekonomii, medycynie i sterowaniu*, Akademicka Oficyna Wydawnicza PLJ, Warszawa, 1999; Z. Pawlak, *Rough Sets. Theoretical Aspects of Reasoning about Data*, Wydawnictwo Politechniki Warszawskiej, Warszawa, 1990; Z. Pawlak, 'Rough Sets', *International Journal of Information and Computer Science*, Vol. 11, No. 341, 1982; Z. Pawlak, 'Zbiory przybliżone nowa matematyczna metoda analizy danych', *in Miesięcznik Politechniki Warszawskiej* No 5/2004. Available at <http://bcpw.bg.pw.edu.pl/Content/1949/zb_przyb.pdf>; Z. Pawlak, K. Słowiński & J. Stefanowski, 'Teoria zbiorów przybliżonych w analizie danych', *in* M. Nałęcz (Ed.), *Biocybernetyka i Inżynieria Biomedyczna*, Vol. 7: Systemy Komputerowe i Teleinformatyczne w Służbie Zdrowia, Akademicka Oficyna Wydawnicza Exit, Warszawa, 2002.

knowledge discovering, complex classification tasks, as well as computer decision support systems. The different characteristics of such a theory ought to be presented in theory and in some practical approaches, given their importance for law. Indeed, rough sets theory, together with algorithms that make use of it, allows analyzing large datasets, enabling the reduction of describing objects features sets to the essential minimum (so-called conditional attribute set reduct). It should be pointed out that the search of applicable law in reality is related to the search of multiple sources. Furthermore, the reconstruction of the meaning of different words relies on a plurality of meanings which shall be reconstructed. Removing data inconsistency if it exists, as well as generating from the data so-called minimal rules, is another important feature. It indeed permits simulating expert activities of disciplines, including law, without neglecting the fundamental constraints, coming from the different fields.[25]

The final part of the syllabus may take into account other aspects such as algorithmic and arithmetic transformation of the language, to permit machine learning of concepts, and their semiotic connection, independently from a specific language,[26] and is therefore specifically fit for the new challenges of law and of legal education. Indeed, lawyers who are accustomed to deal with such methods may be of significant importance in different interdisciplinary teams. Therefore, such a syllabus may support a new kind of legal profession, related to the technological society. An example of such a profession will be given in the next article.

25 Records in the form of If . . . and . . . then . . . *See* Pawlak, Słowiński & Stefanowski 2002. The following are the advantages of rough sets theory: it does not require assumptions concerning the data (*e.g.* probability or fuzziness), it contains fast data analysis algorithms, and it facilitates the interpretation of the results. It has a considerable mathematic simplicity, and therefore appears a method specially fit for interdisciplinary teaching.

26 Nunziante 2005.

15 Legal Training and Legal Profession at the Crossroads with Pharmacology and Telemedicine: Designing a System for Preventing the Circulation of New Psychoactive Substances

Krzysztof Bogusławski, Ornella Corazza and Pasquale Policastro

This article aims to explore the integration of two scientific projects, each with important social implications in the legal training, with special reference to a module on 'Artificial Intelligence and Technological Society'. The first one is the Recreational Drugs European Network (ReDNet) project (<https://www.rednetproject.eu/index.php>), which has been coordinated by the School of Pharmacy of University of Hertfordshire.[1] The aim of the project is to improve the level of information available to young people (from 16 to 24 years old) and professionals on the effects of these new recreational drugs and the potential health risks associated with their use. The second one is 'Telemedicine in Pomerania Region' (<www.telepom.eu/>), a project involving three German regions: Nordbrandenburg, Vorpommern and Westpommern, as well as the Polish Western Pomeranian Region. It also involves three universities: University of Greifswald and Szczecin universities, namely, Pomeranian Medical University and Western Pomeranian Technological University, operating through the Academic Information Centre, as well as over thirty hospitals. Both the projects have been demanding considerable research activity and have been producing a significant quantity of knowledge and skills. For this reason the authors have been trying to join the potential of the two projects in a new approach related to the development of an expert system and a

1 The other associate partners were National Institute of Psychiatry, King's College London; Institute of Psychiatry and Neurology, Warsaw, Poland; Bergen Clinics Foundation, Norway; De Sleutel, Gent, Belgium; Servizio Salute Regione Marche, Ancona, Italy; Consorci Mar Parc de Salut de Barcelona, Spain; Rhine State Hospital, University of Duisberg-Essen, Germany; National Institute of Drug Prevention, Institute for Social Policy and Labour, Budapest, Hungary; DrugScope, London, UK.
The collaborating partners were Eotvos Lorand University, Budapest, Hungary; National Antidrug Agency, Rome, Italy; National Antidrug Agency, Bucharest, Romania; United Nations Office on Drugs and Crime, Vienna, Austria; Adiktologie, Prague, Czech Republic; Children's Society, London, UK; ELISAD, London, UK; State Psychiatric Hospital of Alcohol and Drug Addiction, Sofia, Bulgaria; Trimbos Institute, Utrecht, Netherlands; A-Clinic Foundation, Helsinki, Finland; Institute for Research and Development 'Utrip', Grosuplje, Slovenia; University of Szczecin, Poland; Dipartimento Dipendenze Patologiche di Macerata, Italytimento Dipendenze Patologiche di Macerata, Italy.

decision supporting system to analyze the trends in the development and the consumption of novel psychoactive substances (NPS). In this new attempt the authors have been joined by other partners, namely, the European Master in Law and Policies of European Integration: European Constitutional Law and Multilevel Constitutionalism, the consortium ECONET, the Centre of Technology and Knowledge Transfer of Szczecin University, the Department of Constitutional Law and European Integration of the Faculty of Law and Administration, as well as the Department of System Designing of the Faculty of Economics and Management of the said university of Szczecin.

Joining the potential of research of the participants to contribute to the solution to an important problem such as production and distribution of NPS has further implications for legal education. Indeed, one of the many interesting debates that have been developing together with the project 'Menu for Justice – Toward a European Curriculum Studiorum on Judicial Studies' is that the present transformations of the social, political and economic conditions have been generating new calls and new needs for the legal profession. In particular, it has been highlighted that the needs of court administration require specific knowledge and training which embody a new kind of legal profession.[2] In this article we show that the coordination of the potentials of ReDNet project and 'Telemedicine in Western Pomerania Region', while giving the opportunity to obtain a survey on the territory concerning the trends in the consumption of NPS, responding to the need of different actors and different public services, such as public health, security, instruction, requires a deciding role of the lawyers working within interdisciplinary teams. The participation of the lawyers concerns compliance and legislation making and appears of significant complexity such as envisaging new approaches to legal professions in the technological society, as well as justifying the relevance of the participation to the designing and operation of the project as part of a syllabus of a module of 'Artificial Intelligence and Technological Society'.

The last ten years have seen a rapid change in the social, cultural, legal and political contexts of the illicit drug market, which has led to unpredictable challenges to the point where in their 2011 report the UN International Narcotic Control Board (INCB) declared that designer drug production and distribution was 'out of control'. During the past years of activity, the ReDNet project was able to identify more than 650 novel products and combinations about which there is very little scientific knowledge. These products are of particular concern as they are advertised online as 'legal' and 'pure', making them more attractive to abusers, mainly young people. More specifically they are (1) not approved for human consumption and thus might well have unknown pharmacological effects and unpredictable

2 Chapter 9, Philip Langbroek, Court Administration as a Practice and as an Academic Discipline.

side effects and adverse reactions on users; (2) legal and thus perceived as safe by actual or potential users; (3) often sold as something else, like mystical incenses, plant chemicals and bath salts; (4) unknown to health and other professionals who constantly need to receive updated and accurate information about these new substances; (5) unknown most of the time also in the scientific literature; (6) increasingly accepted as part of a lifestyle rather than being considered as a misuse of drugs; (7) just a 'click away' from our homes and thus potentially available to everyone, especially young people, who are amongst the most at risk in taking advantage of information and products available online.

In this context of sudden change, novel legal responses are essential to tackle this rapidly expanding illicit market. According to the preamble to the recommendation of EU Council, EU Drugs Strategy (2013-20),[3]

> 5. The drugs phenomenon is a national and international issue that needs to be addressed in a global context. In this regard, coordinated action carried out at EU level plays an important role. [. . .] By providing a framework for joint and complementary actions, the Strategy ensures that resources invested in this area are used effectively and efficiently, whilst taking into account the institutional and financial constraints and capacities of Member States and of the EU institutions.

At present, the main problem for lawmakers is to try and stay ahead of the chemists who are devising new drugs to be outside the law. This, of course, is very difficult; nevertheless, some countries have introduced new, more generic legislations which try to capture new drugs and all subsequent drugs from the same 'family'. This has happened, for example, in the UK, where the idea of temporary orders has also been introduced. In this case, a drug that looks as if it might be dangerous is temporarily banned while a scientific investigation is carried out. However, the challenge to find new and more harmonized legislative solutions at different national and international levels still remains open.

In response to this phenomenon, the ReDNet project intends to explore the potential of a number of innovative information communication technologies (ITCs *e.g.* texting, social networking sites, Second Life and other multimedia platforms) in the timely dissemination of accurate and non-judgemental evidence-based information in line with the needs of each target group. ReDNet aims to (1) develop accurate information on NPS, (2) develop and pilot a variety of innovative and effective ICTs to disseminate this information, (3) access the feasibility of different ICTs and the relevance of the information being disseminated

3 Official Journal of the European Union 29 December 2012: 2012/C 402/01.

to the target groups and (4) inform future technology-based research in health education and prevention.

Particularly successful so far was the new SMS/email information service (SMAIL), a new mobile/web tool created to help people to keep up to date about the new trends in drug use. The service is part of the ReDNet project activities and is available internationally (in English). It is easy to use and free of charge (<www.rednetproject/smail>). The system enables registered users (1) to receive regular emails/messages that contain fact sheets with scientifically based information on the nature and the risks of NPSs; (2) to receive regular SMS/emails that contain invitations to events; (3) to send SMS with a drug name that automatically responds with either an SMS or email containing more information and (4) to send email with a drug name that automatically responds with either an SMS or email containing more information.[4] The importance of the data presented should, however, be considered, taking into account the effort to guarantee the maximum positive impact on human rights, both in collecting and in disseminating the data. The recommendation of the Council on EU Drug Strategy 2013-2020 points out the following in its preamble:

> 2. This Drugs Strategy is based first and foremost on the fundamental principles of EU law and, in every regard, upholds the founding values of the Union: respect for human dignity, liberty, democracy, equality, solidarity, the rule of law and human rights. It aims to protect and improve the well-being of society and of the individual, to protect public health, to offer a high level of security for the general public and to take a balanced, integrated and evidence-based approach to the drugs phenomenon.

This aspect calls for an approach to the flow of information which may permit adequate compliance with legal standards and adequate monitoring that address the development and implementation of best practices in the field of human rights protection and implementation.

Telemedicine may give important technical contribution to attain the said task. It combines indeed medical services and health care with elements of telecommunications, IT and medicine. Using this new technology allows to break down geographical barriers, permitting the exchange of specialized information. So far this has been used by sending static and dynamic images (high-quality radiographs, electrocardiography, ultrasound,

---

4 O. Corazza *et al.*, 'Promoting innovation and excellence to face the rapid diffusion of novel psychoactive substances (NPS) in the EU: the outcomes of the ReDNet project', *in Human Psychopharmacology: Clinical and Experimental*, 2013 (in press). *See also* O. Corazza *et al.*, 'Novel Drugs, Novel Solutions: Exploring the Potential of Technological Tools for Prevention of Drug Abuse', *Italian Journal of Addiction*, Vol. 1, Nos. 1-2, 2011, pp. 25-30.

magnetic resonance imaging). For drug prevention, the properly managed flow of data concerning public and social behaviours, school and work behaviours, water analyses and medical observation, on a regional scale, may permit significant progress. So far, telemedicine is widely used in different ambits and permits the best joining of different abilities, especially for diagnostic purposes. These characteristics may therefore be extended. Modern technology indeed, which uses fast processors and algorithms for digital signal processing and compression, enables transferring high-resolution images and interactive audiovisual, real-time transmission with exceptional accuracy. This makes the telemedicine tools able to be adapted for a number of uses. Furthermore, information technology (IT) permits that hospitals may operate multiple systems concerning telemedicine. The main system is called Hospital Information System (HIS). Another system is a RIS (Radiology Information System), which deals with the work of doctors who support radiologists. Image data are stored in the archive PACS (picture archiving and communication systems). In the project 'Telemedicine in Western Pomerania Region', the starting point was to define an interface for the exchange of medical data and in particular the imaging data between hospitals to perform remote diagnostics activities. The solution developed forms a system, in the sense that it makes use of a set of cooperating protocols. This reason justified the denomination of Medical Expertise Ordering System (MEDEOS). This name refers mainly to the primary goal of operation of the said system, *i.e.* electronic ordering of interpretations of radiologic examinations, but due to its flexibility, the System may perform other functions in the future as well.

The key principles of MEDEOS are as follows: simplicity – simple systems can be implemented at a low cost and are easy to maintain, flexibility – to allow realization of new functions based on the same mechanism and security, which is required when transmitting sensitive personal data.

15.1 Elements of the System

The importance of these principles is that their use may permit to develop an overall control of the system by means of compliance to legal rules.

The evolution which we are envisaging is the use of MEDEOS for an application making use of an artificial intelligence (AI) approach for a system that addresses the Prevention of the Evolutions of New Substances Extensively Interfering in the Personal Development (PENSIERO).[5] The system aims at studying trends and evolutionary patterns on a regional

5 In Polish: Prewencja Ewolucji Nowych Substancji Ingerujących Ekstensywnie w Rozwój Osobisty (PENSIERO).

basis, as well as supporting decision-making. It may join different subjects, who develop models of descriptions of relevant issues for drug consumption. They include subjects who establish which information has to be collected and their form, subjects who collect information, and subjects who interpret information. In this way, a decision supporting system may permit to make full use of three different functions of law: prevention, control and sanctions. These aspects represent a kind of new potential since the consolidated approach to New Drugs; for example, the Council decision 2005/387/JHA of 10 May 2005 on the information exchange, risk assessment and control of NPSs appeared to be a typical one aimed at affecting structural variables, with the aim to reach sanction purposes.[6] The participation of law students in its development appears to be a significant part of a syllabus that addresses 'Legal Applications in the Technological Society', which is a strong spillover into the skills to adapt legal knowledge in the field of constitutional law, administrative law and human rights to complex technological activities.

A fundamental task of the expert system would be, first, to consider the correlation of highly heterogeneous elements, connected with the phenomenology of the problem. The presence of lawyers from the moment of projecting the system would be very important for creating a demand of knowledge, needed to support the skills to deal with difficult and sometimes unpredictable problems and to operate in a context where different actors have different aims and needs, which nevertheless influence the legally relevant sphere of the addresses.[7] This possibility to interact with the making of this project happens to be a very good occasion for training different skills, in particular for lawyers.

The protection of individual rights and freedoms is indeed the final aim of the system. We shall take into account the positive legal data of the "respect for human dignity, liberty,

---

6 *See* P. Policastro, 'Promoting a Multidisciplinary Approach to Develop New Drug Legislation: Its Practical Meaning for the European Legislation', keynote speech at the ReDNet project, European Conference on Novel Psychoactive Substances, Budapest, 12-13 March 2012.

7 *See* the Recommendation of the European Parliament and of the Council of 23 April 2008 on the establishment of the European Qualifications Framework (EQF) for lifelong learning Official Journal C111, 6 May 2008, P. 0001-0007. In Annex II, the descriptors defining levels in the EQF are indicated. At Levels 6 and 7, which are especially important for master's studies, we have the following: Level 6 [**] – the learning outcomes relevant to Level 6 are advanced knowledge in a field of work or study [. . .]; advanced skills, demonstrating mastery and innovation, required to solve complex and unpredictable problems in a specialized field of work or study; management of complex technical or professional activities or projects, taking responsibility for decision-making [. . .] and responsibility for managing professional development of individuals and groups.
Level 7 [***] – the learning outcomes relevant to Level 7 are highly specialized knowledge, some of which is at the forefront of knowledge in a field of work or study, as the basis for original thinking and/or research; critical awareness of knowledge issues in a field and at the interface between different fields; specialized problem-solving skills required in research and/or innovation [. . .] and to integrate knowledge from different fields; management and transformation of work or study contexts that are complex, unpredictable and require new strategic approaches [. . .].

democracy, equality, solidarity, the rule of law and human rights", stressed in the above-mentioned Recommendation of the Council 'EU Drugs Strategy (2013-20)', which furthermore stresses the importance of "coordinated [...] joint and complementary actions". Therefore, the accomplishment of public duties by means of the system shall be addressed, in a way beyond any possible doubt, not only to implement the known values and standards but also highlighting new dangers and incongruences and to promote new best practices, also by means of legislation. Furthermore, we have the aspects related to the different understandings of the implementation of the protection of human rights and the constitutional values from the point of view of the different actors and the different public duties. The degree of complexity of such multiple understandings is augmented when the legal culture of different countries interact in the system, as it has already been experienced in the 'Telemedicine in Western Pomerania' project. For this reason, the discussion with the legal students and scholars within a specialized research team addressed to consider all the issues involved may lead to several master's theses and, eventually, to PhD dissertations. It may produce a significant feedback affecting the training also at vocational level (Level 5).

These reasons justify the integration of such a project when designing a module on 'Artificial Intelligence and Technological Society' for a Master diploma based upon the experience of the European Master in Law and Policies of European Integration: European Constitutional Law and Multilevel Constitutionalism.[8]

Indeed, according to the recommendation of an EQF for the corresponding levels of higher education (Levels 6 and 7), at least the following are required: a critical understanding, mastery and innovation in solving unpredictable problems adapted to contexts, which require new strategic approaches (Level 6). Level 7 requires even more, among other things: critical awareness of knowledge issues in a field and at the interface between different fields, specialized problem-solving skills required in research and/or innovation in order to develop new knowledge and procedures and to integrate knowledge from different fields, ability to manage and transform work or study contexts that are complex, unpredictable and require new strategic approaches. The participation in the designing and operation of a project as the present ones may be significantly addressed to achieve these goals, and this justifies its inclusion in the syllabus for Artificial Intelligence and

8 On this subject, we may remember the exercise performed by the students of the European Master in Law and Policies of European Integration: European Constitutional Law and Multilevel Constitutionalism in 2010 (under the coordination of P. Policastro), to formulate some reflection on a directive on the 'Harmonization measures and the programmes to develop an integrated approach to social communication, developing citizens' culture and attitude at any age and condition, in particular to prevent and to fight the commerce and use of substances for the purpose of "recreational drugs", and the consumption of recreational drugs, including, but not only, the "spice" and other related synthetic cannabinoids'.

Technological Society, addressing legal training. The experience obtained from the practice of students in law from France and Poland in the project ReDNet[9] confirms such a statement. Furthermore, such a perspective may eventually support the development of a continuum between master's and PhD training.

The recent emergence of new designer drugs, also known as novel psychoactive substances (NPS), combined with the ability of the Internet to disseminate information quickly and act as an online marketplace, has raised concerns across drug and health policy, legislation and research. Both the number of largely unregulated substances and the rapidity with which they appear and evolve have led to challenges for governments, professionals and (potential) users alike. For this reason, the development of PENSIERO system appears specially fit for legal training in an interdisciplinary context, as well as the training in other related professions (information specialists, technology experts, physicians, police and public security experts, teachers, public administrators, *etc*). This will allow the best respect for the constitutional principles, starting from human rights. In this sense the envisaged activity aims to support a multidisciplinary training based upon the implementation of the principles of compliance regarding constitutional law and human rights, for the control of the illicit drug market and the intervention against the circulation of NPS. For this reason, it may permit to train also specialists in other fields regarding questions of compliance. At the same time, it may allow to highlight the importance of law and of specially trained lawyers to deal efficiently with the compliance, with the development of an adequate legislative language to deal with the rapidity of change, and the development of growingly sophisticated practices for the best protection of the person.

9 Coordinated with the practices of 'The European Master in Law and Policies of European Integration: European Constitutional Law and Multilevel Constitutionalism', see *supra* T. Freixes and P. Policastro.

About the Authors

Pasquale Policastro, editor, pasquale@mec.univ.szczecin.pl, PhD hab. in Law, Professor of Constitutional Law and European Integration at Szczecin University, Director of the European Master in Law and Policies of European Integration: European Constitutional Law and Multilevel Constitutionalism (together with Teresa Freixes – director-in-chief Barcelona, Paola Bilancia – Milano, Alexandre Viala – Montpellier), Secretary General (together with Emilio Castorina) of ECONET, Centre of Research and Advanced Training of European Constitutional Law.

Marek Andrzejewski, andrzejewski.marek@wp.pl, PhD hab. in Law, Professor, Szczecin University; Head of the Centre of Family Law and Rights of the Child, Polish Academy of Sciences.

Rainer Arnold, jean.monnet@gmx.de, PhD in Law, professor emeritus at the University of Regensburg, Germany.

Andrzej Bałaban, a.balaban@o2.pl, PhD hab. in Law, Professor, Head of the Department of Constitutional Law, Faculty of Law and Administration, Szczecin University; State University of Applied Science, Gorzów Wielkopolski, Poland.

Bogusław Banaszak, PhD hab. in Law, Dr. h.c. mult., Head of the Department of Constitutional Law, Faculty of Law, Administration and Economics, University of Wrocław, Poland.

Tomas Berkmanas, t.berkmanas@tf.vdu.lt, PhD in Law, Associate Professor, Vice-Dean for Research, Faculty of Law, Vytautas Magnus University Kaunas, Lithuania.

Krzysztof Bogusławski, kbogu@man.szczecin.pl, PhD. in technological sciences, Faculty of Computer Science and Information Systems, Head of the Academic Centre of Information, West Pomeranian University of Technology in Szczecin.

Emilio Castorina, ecastorina@lex.unict.it, PhD in Law, Professor of Constitutional Law, Department 'Legal Seminar', University of Catania, Secretary General (together with Pasquale Policastro) of ECONET, Centre of Research and Advanced Training of European Constitutional Law.

Ornella Corazza, o.corazza@herts.ac.uk, PhD, University of London, School of Oriental and African Studies, Principal Lecturer in Mental Health and Research Manager at University of Hertfordshire.

Teresa Freixes, tfreixes@telefonica.net, PhD in Law, Professor of Constitutional Law, University Autonoma of Barcelona (UAB), Head of the Chair Jean Monnet 'ad personam' in European constitutional law, President of the University Foundation Martí l'Humà, Director of the Centre of Studies in Human Rights (UAB), Director-in-chief of the European Master in Law and Policies of European Integration: European Constitutional Law and Multilevel Constitutionalism (together with Pasquale Policastro – Szczecin, Paola Bilancia – Milano, Alexandre Viala – Montpellier), senior expert of the Agency of Fundamental Rights of the European Union and of the European Institute of Gender Equality.

Ole Hammerslev, ohv@sam.sdu.dk, PhD in Sociology, Professor, Head of Studies, Department of Law, University of Southern Denmark.

İbrahim Ö. Kaboğlu, ibrahimkaboglu@yahoo.fr, PhD in Law agr., Professor, Head of the Chair of Constitutional Law, Marmara University, Istanbul, Turkey. Visiting professor at the University of Limoges, Head of the editorial board *Anayasa Hukuku Dergisi/Journal of Constitutional Law/Revue de droit constitutionnel.*

Philip Langbroek, p.m.langbroek@uu.nl, PhD in Law, Professor of Justice Administration and Judicial Organization, Chair of the Institute for Jurisprudence, Constitutional and Administrative Law at the Montaigne Centre of Utrecht Law School, Utrecht, the Netherlands.

Luigi Lepore, lepore@uniparthenope.it, PhD in Law, Assistant Professor and Researcher of Business Administration and Public Management, Department of Business Administration and Public Management, Parthenope University of Naples – Italy.

Bartosz Makowicz, b.makowicz@uni-muenster.de, PhD in Law, Professor of Law at the European University Viadrina Frankfurt (Oder) – Faculty of Law, and Scientific Director at the Compliance Academy (<www.ca-seminare.de>).

Kesra Nermend, kesra@wneiz.pl, PhD hab. in Technological and Information Sciences, Head of the Chair of System Design, Faculty of Economics and Management, Szczecin University; Head of the Centre of Technology Transfer, Szczecin University.

Mateusz Piwowarski, mpiwowarski@ps.pl, PhD in Technological Sciences, Assistant Professor, Institute of Information System, Western Pomeranian Technological University, Szczecin.

Agata Wawrzyniak, agataw@wneiz.pl, PhD in Economic Sciences, Assistant Professor, Institute of Information Technologies in Management, Faculty of Economics and Management, Szczecin University.

Barbara Wąsikowska, barbara.wasikowska@wneiz.pl, PhD in Economic Sciences, Assistant Professor, Institute of Information Technologies in Management, Faculty of Economics and Management, Szczecin University.